EXPLORING OUR WORLD WITH MAPS

Map Skills for Grades K–6

HAIG A. RUSHDOONY

Fearon Teacher Aids
Carthage, Illinois

Dedicated to Jon, Kathy, Jim, Karen, and Jimmy

ACKNOWLEDGMENTS

Maps 8, 9, 15, and 27 reprinted, by permission, from the United States Geological Survey.

Map 16, population data, supplied by the United States Department of Commerce Bureau of Census.

Maps 17, 18, 25A, and 25B reprinted, by permission, from the United States Department of Agriculture.

Photos 1 and 2, for Map 5, reprinted, by permission, from *The Language of Maps*.

Photos 3 and 4 reprinted, by permission, from the Photographic Division, NASA, Houston.

ISBN 0-8224-4396-1

Printed in the United States of America

1. 9 8 7 6

Contents

Preface   v

Introduction   1

PART I   Teacher-Directed Lessons   3

DISCOVERING OUR ENVIRONMENT   4

Unit 1   Orienting Ourselves in the Classroom   5

Unit 2   Orienting Ourselves Outside   7

Unit 3   Determining Directions and Distances   9

Unit 4   Making a Map of Our School   11

Unit 5   Making a Map of Our Classroom   13

EXPLORING OUR ENVIRONMENT   14

Unit 6   Orienting Ourselves to the Environment   15

Unit 7   Comparing Two Different Maps   17

Unit 8   Making a Map of Our Neighborhood   19

Unit 9   Examining a Globe of the Earth   21

Unit 10   Comparing Maps and Globes   23

GOING BEYOND OUR ENVIRONMENT   24

Unit 11   Comparing Maps and Photos   25

Unit 12   Comparing Road Maps   27

Unit 13   Determining Size and Shape   30

Unit 14   Introducing Height and Elevation   33

Unit 15   Making a Relief Map   35

DISCOVERING OUR REGION AND NATION   36

Unit 16   Examining Maps of the United States   37

Unit 17   Comparing Different Ways to Show Scale   39

Unit 18   Exploring United States Time Zones   43

Unit 19   Exploring Elevation   46

Unit 20   Using Distribution Maps   47

EXPLORING THE WORLD AROUND US   49

Unit 21   Using Contour Lines   50

Unit 22   Orienting Ourselves to the World   53

Unit 23   Determining Global Distances   59

Unit 24   Interpreting Different Types of Maps   61

Unit 25   Orienting Ourselves from Space   63

PART II   Self-Directed Activities   65

DISCOVERING OUR ENVIRONMENT ACTIVITIES

Activity 1   Knowing Directions   66
Activity 2   What's the Picture?   67
Activity 3   Find the Directions!   68
Activity 4   Finding Your Way Around School   69
Activity 5   Using Symbols   70

EXPLORING OUR ENVIRONMENT ACTIVITIES

Activity 6   Knowing How to Orient Yourself   71
Activity 7   Using Keys to Unlock Maps   72
Activity 8   Finding Places at the Zoo   73
Activity 9   Making Your Own Semantic Map   75
Activity 10   A Picture Clue Crossword Puzzle   76

GOING BEYOND OUR ENVIRONMENT ACTIVITIES

Activity 11   Finding Places on a Road Map   77
Activity 12   Finding Distances on a Road Map   79
Activity 13   Comparing Shapes and Sizes   81
Activity 14   Exploring Landforms in South America   83
Activity 15   Using Map Terms: A Crossword Puzzle   84

DISCOVERING OUR REGION AND NATION ACTIVITIES

Activity 16   A Map Word Search   86
Activity 17   Working with Scale and Distance   87
Activity 18   Finding States on a United States Map:
                A Word Puzzle   88
Activity 19   Matching Cross Sections and Word
                Descriptions   90
Activity 20   Using Maps to Gather Information   91

EXPLORING THE WORLD AROUND US

Activity 21   Getting to the Top with Cross Sections and
                Contours   93
Activity 22   Finding Places Using Longitude and Latitude   95
Activity 23   Drawing Conclusions from Different Sources   97
Activity 24   Exploring Different Maps   98
Activity 25   Filling in the Blanks: A Crossword Puzzle   100

MAP OF CANADA   102

PART III   Answer Key   103

PART IV   Maps and Photos   107

Preface

Geographic illiteracy is running rampant in this country. Studies have shown that Americans—young and old, educated and not—are appallingly ignorant about geography. I witnessed a telling example of this several months after the Grenada incident. I was attending a conference on teaching global concepts and skills. The leader of one session, who was there to help us update our knowledge on global interdependence, did not know where Grenada is!

The purpose of this book is two-fold—to help your students develop the ability to locate places on maps and globes, and to help them become more aware of their relationship with this planet and their environment. The map skills and concepts that appear in this book were drawn from currently used social studies textbooks. Therefore, the activities and lessons will complement your social studies curriculum, giving your students a greater understanding of the map skills and geography they are learning.

Part I contains 25 structured, teacher-directed units with objectives, material lists, lesson procedures, and follow-up activities. Part II contains 25 self-directed student activities and map exercises. Hopefully, as you introduce the lessons and activities, you will find that your students have an increased desire to discover and explore the world of maps.

Haig A. Rushdoony

Introduction

This book is divided into four parts. Part I contains teacher-directed lessons. Part II contains self-directed activities. Part III is the answer key, and Part IV includes the numbered maps and photos that are used with Parts I and II. Parts I and II contain parallel sections—Discovering Our Environment, Exploring Our Environment, Going Beyond Our Environment, Discovering Our Region and Nation, and Exploring the World Around Us—to be used together. Each of these sections is recommended for certain grades. However, these are only suggestions. Since the units are sequential within the book, you can pick and choose activities that are most appropriate for your students' skill levels.

Using Part I

Part I contains the teaching units that will help you teach basic map skills. Each unit contains precise lesson plans that are developed sequentially. These lessons should be used in order within each unit. However, the lessons can be taught on different days.

Each unit also contains the following parts: an objective, a materials list, and a vocabulary list. The *objective* indicates the skills to be learned in the unit. The *materials* section tells you what you will need for each lesson. It is assumed that the following materials—a chalkboard, chalk, an overhead projector, pencils, and paper—are readily available, so they are not listed in the materials. The *vocabulary* list contains words that are introduced in the unit.

Using Part II

The activities in Part II are designed to reinforce the teacher-directed lessons. These reproducible worksheets may be used as a follow-up to the corresponding teacher unit, or at the end of the appropriate teacher section. The activities focus on maps skills while giving practice in the basic skills of reading, writing, and arithmetic.

If any of your students have difficulty doing the activities, you may wish to consider one of the following alternatives: 1) read the activity aloud and work through it cooperatively with a small group; 2) have students work in pairs; 3) record the activities on tapes or cassettes and allow the students to work through them with the accompanying visuals.

Using Parts III and IV

The answer key in Part III contains the answers to all the group activities and self-directed activities. You might want to read the answers aloud, so students can correct their own work.

The maps and photos in Part IV are used with the teacher-directed lessons and the self-directed lessons. The materials list for each unit indicates whether you will need transparencies and/or reproductions of each visual.

Additional Resources

For those of you desiring additional background and resources, two short but timely resources are *Maps: A Historical Survey of Their Study and Collecting,* Illustrated Edition, by R.A. Skelton (Chicago: University of Chicago Press, 1975) and *The Map Catalog: Every Kind of Map and Chart on Earth and Even Some Above It* edited by Joel Makower (New York: Vantage Books, A Division of Random Books, 1986). These books are filled with a variety of maps which you may wish to use or have for your more interested youngsters.

Two additional books (published by Fearon Teacher Aids, a division of David S. Lake Publishers) will provide supplement to and will complement this book. They are *Marvelous Maps and Graphs: Practical Worksheets for Grades 1–3* by Ginger Wentrcek (1984) and *The Language of Maps* by Haig A. Rushdoony.

PART I
Teacher-Directed Lessons

DISCOVERING OUR ENVIRONMENT

(Suggested for Grades K–1)

Unit 1 Orienting Ourselves in the Classroom
Lesson 1.1   Using left, right, up, and down
Lesson 1.2   Using north, south, east, and west
Follow-Up

Unit 2 Orienting Ourselves Outside
Lesson 2.1   Using the sun
Lesson 2.2   Using shadows and shadow sticks
Lesson 2.3   Using a compass
Follow-Up

Unit 3 Determining Directions and Distances
Lesson 3.1   On a neighborhood walk
Lesson 3.2   Inside the classroom
Follow-Up

Unit 4 Making a Map of Our School
Lesson 4.1   Introducing a simple school map
Lesson 4.2   Making a map of the school
Lesson 4.3   Using a map of the school
Follow-Up

Unit 5 Making a Map of Our Classroom
Lesson 5   Making the map
Follow-Up

UNIT 1 *Orienting Ourselves in the Classroom*

Objective:	To identify and distinguish between left, right, up, down, north, south, east, and west.
Materials:	classroom objects; manila strips with north, south, east, and west printed on them; large photos, pictures, slides, or transparencies (for Follow-Up)
Vocabulary:	left; right; up; down; north; south; east; west; in between; next to

LESSON 1.1 Using left, right, up, and down

1. Begin the lesson by playing a game called "Who is It?" Ask questions using the words *left, right,* and *in between.* For instance, you could ask, "Who is sitting to the *left* of Ann?" or "Who is sitting to the *right* of Jose?" You should also ask the children to identify a child sitting in between two children. Make sure the children answer the questions with the child's name.

2. When children grasp the idea of the game, let a child who correctly identifies another child be "IT." Have "IT" ask the questions until another child answers correctly.

3. After the children are familiar with each other's names and the first set of words, vary the game by playing "What is It?" Use the words *up, down,* and *next to,* and ask questions such as, "What is *up* on the left wall?" "What is *down* on the floor?" "What is *next to* the poster on the right wall?" When the children are comfortable playing the game, have children who answer correctly be "IT."

4. Sum up the lesson by asking the children to review the terms they used in the game. You might also ask the children if they learned any names they did not know or if they found things in the classroom that they weren't previously aware of.

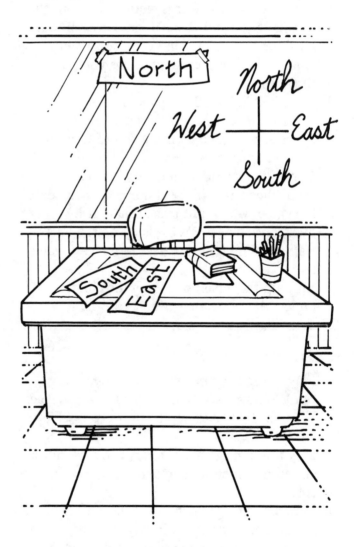

UNIT 1 continued

LESSON 1.2   Using north, south, east, and west

(Note: You may wish to introduce Unit 2—
Orienting Ourselves Outside—before teaching
this lesson. This will give children experience
with finding actual directions outside.)

1. On the chalkboard make a large chart that
   shows the four cardinal (main) directions (see
   Figure 1). Explain that these are four main
   directions—north, south, east, and west. Have
   the class read the words aloud. Then put the
   manila strips on the walls (one on each wall—
   north on the wall behind your desk). Have the
   children repeat the directions as you put
   them up.
2. Play the "Who is It?" game in Lesson 1.1
   using *north, south, east,* and *west* in your
   questions—"Who is sitting *east* of Cecelia?"
   "Who is sitting to the *north* of Brian?"
   Continue playing until the children understand the terms. If the children quickly learn
   the game, you might make it harder by asking
   questions such as "What is up on the north
   wall?" "Who is sitting next to the east wall?"
   and so on.
3. Sum up the lesson by asking the children to
   review the terms they used in the game.

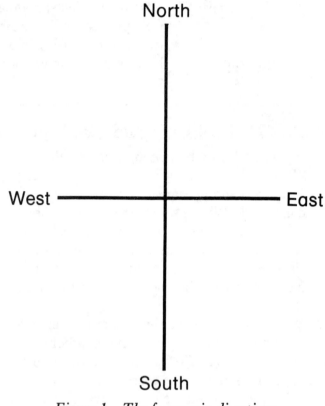

Figure 1   *The four main directions*

FOLLOW-UP

1. Play the same game, but vary it by asking
   riddle questions—"I am to the left of Michael.
   Who am I?" "I am on the north wall. What
   am I?"
2. Play the same game, but vary it by asking the
   children to identify items in the classroom by
   color.
3. Play the same game, but vary it by having the
   children identify items in large photos,
   pictures, slides, or transparencies. (This is a
   good way to introduce orientation of maps.)

UNIT 2   *Orienting Ourselves Outside*

Objective:	To identify the four cardinal directions outdoors.
Materials:	yardstick or similar stick; magnetic compass; 18″ × 36″ oaktag; large marker; 2 large pieces of butcher paper
Vocabulary:	northern; southern; eastern; western; opposite; compass
Note:	If you are living in the Southern Hemisphere, the directions in these lessons will be reversed.

LESSON 2.1   Using the sun

1. Review the cardinal directions introduced in Lesson 1.2 (page 6).
2. On a sunny day tell the children that you are going to take them outside to observe the position of the sun. Take them outside at the beginning of the day, at noon, and at the end of the day. Each time have the children observe the position of the sun. Make sure you emphasize that we should never look directly at the sun. Point out that the sun appears in the *eastern* part of the sky in the morning, *overhead* at noon, and in the *western* part of the sky in the afternoon.
3. Repeat this activity for the next day or two until the children grasp the idea that the sun appears to be in different parts of the sky at different times. You might help them out by asking questions such as, "Did we see the sun in the same place in the sky in the morning as we did in the afternoon?" Encourage the children to look at the sun's apparent location on their way to and from school.
4. Play a game outside. Have two children stand back-to-back—one facing the sun. Point out that the children are facing *opposite* directions. Ask the children questions using the vocabulary words. For example, "Who is facing *north*?" "Who is facing the *opposite* of north?" "What is the opposite of north?" Repeat with other children and directions.

LESSON 2.2   Using shadows and shadow sticks

1. On the oaktag, make a chart that tells the children how to orient themselves at noon on a sunny day (see Figure 2). Hold up the chart and read the information to the class. Tell the children that today the class will see how well they can find directions outside at noon.
2. Take the class outside and have the children stand with the sun at their backs. Point out that the children's shadows face away from the sun or to the north.
3. Hold up the chart for the class to see and reread the information. Ask the children to point to the north, east, south, and west.
4. Have the children move to a different place and reorient themselves. Again have them point out the different directions. You might want to vary the activity by asking questions such as, "What direction is to your right?"
5. Repeat the activity using a shadow stick. Hold the yardstick so it is perpendicular to the ground. Point out to the children that the stick's shadow points in the same direction as our shadows do. Have the children find the directions until they are comfortable using both their shadows and the shadow sticks.

Finding Directions at Noon
Stand with your back to the sun.
You are facing north.
East is to your right.
West is to your left.
South is in back of you.

Figure 2   Finding the directions at noon

UNIT 2 continued

LESSON 2.3   Using a compass

1. Review the previous lesson. Ask children if they think they could do this activity if it were a cloudy day. Explain that one way to find directions if it is not sunny is to use a *compass*.

2. Draw a picture of a compass on the chalkboard. Tell children that this is a picture of a compass. Explain that the needle on the compass always points to the magnetic north pole. Place the compass on a piece of butcher paper marked with directional lines (but not the directions). Turn the compass until north matches a line. Mark the line with an N. (See Figure 3.) Ask the children to look at the compass and help you mark the other lines. Then ask them to point in the different directions.

3. When it is cloudy, take the children outside and repeat step 2.

4. Review the different ways in which we can find directions.

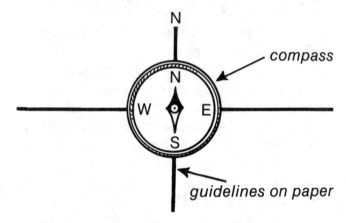

Figure 3   Orienting compass on paper

FOLLOW-UP

1. Shortly before noon, on a sunny day, take the class on a schoolyard or neighborhood walk. As the children walk, give directions such as, "Turn east at the corner." Point out that the children need to use their shadows or shadow sticks to find their way.

2. During the physical education period, play a game called *Direction Relay*. Divide the class into two teams, choosing one child to be the "direction." Have the teams line up so the children's backs face the sun, and have the "direction" child stand some distance away, facing the sun. (See Figure 4.) Score the game in the following manner:
   - One point for the team of the child who touches the "direction's" outstretched hand first.
   - One point for the team of the child who correctly identifies the location of the "direction" (for example, at noon, the direction child is *north* of the team).

If you have time, play the game again with a new "direction" child. This time have the teams line up with their right or left sides to the sun.

● Direction
  Child

1 2 3 4 5 6 7 8   8 7 6 5 4 3 2 1
Team 1   Team 2

sun

Figure 4   Direction Relay

UNIT 3 *Determining Directions and Distances*

Objective:	To locate places and compute distances on a neighborhood walk and in a simulation game.
Materials:	manila strips with north, south, east, and west printed on them
Vocabulary:	close (closer, closest); far (farther, farthest); shortest route

LESSON 3.1   On a neighborhood walk

1. Review how to use the sun at noon to find the main directions. (See Lesson 2.2, page 7.)

2. Shortly before noon, on a sunny day, take the class on a neighborhood walk. Have the class choose a direction in which to walk, for example, east. Help the children orient themselves. Then ask if any of the children live in that direction. (If none do, you should pick a different direction.) Have those children come to the front of the line.

3. Start walking and have the children count the number of blocks the class travels. (If your school is in an area that doesn't have blocks, you should use a simple pedometer to measure the distance in parts of a mile.) When you pass a child's house, explain that this child lives *closest* to the school. When you pass another child's house, use the vocabulary words to compare the distance of the two houses from the school. For instance, you might say, "Mary lives closer to the school than David," or "David lives *farther* from the school than Mary." Continue walking and pointing out comparisons until you feel the children understand the terms. (Note: You may want or need to repeat this lesson on another day. If you do, have the children walk in a different direction.)

4. Return to the classroom and review the walk. Ask questions such as, "Who lived closest to the school?" "Who lived in between Aaron's house and Betsy's house?" "How many blocks away from the school was Joey's house?"

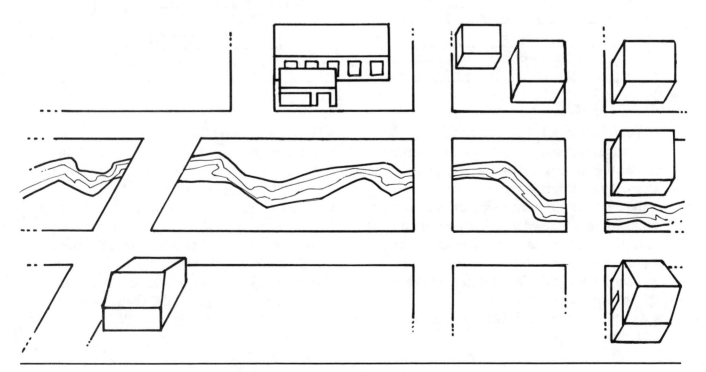

UNIT 3 continued

LESSON 3.2 Inside the classroom

1. Play a simulation game called "My Town." Before class, arrange the desks in one of the ways shown in Figure 5. Put up the manila signs, with the sign reading "north" on the north wall. (If necessary, use a compass to determine north.)

2. Review the main directions with the class. Then explain to the children that each desk (or group of desks) represents one block (if you live in a town) or one mile (if you live in a rural area). Tell the children that you will pick one child to be a "visitor" and another child to be a "friend." The visitor will walk from his or her house (desk) to the house (desk) of the friend. Explain that as the visitor travels, he or she should tell the rest of the class the direction in which he or she is moving and the turns that he or she makes (left or right). When the visitor reaches the friend's desk, the visitor should also tell the class the distance that he or she walked.

3. Call on one child. Tell him or her to visit another child. Have both stand for everyone to see. Ask the visitor to begin, making sure that he or she names the cardinal directions, left and right turns, and the distance as he or she walks.

4. Have the visitor return home, again noting directions, turns, and distance. Point out that the distance doesn't change, but the directions and the turns are reversed.

5. Repeat the game with other children.

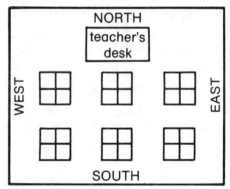

Figure 5   Possible arrangements of desks for "My Town"

FOLLOW-UP

1. Repeat Lesson 3.1. Record the time when you leave and return. Then, on another day, repeat the same walk without stopping. Discuss the differences between the two walks. You might want to ask questions such as, "Would it take a longer or shorter amount of time to ride the same number of blocks on a bike?"

2. Repeat Lesson 3.2. Vary the game in one of the following ways:
   • Ask the children to find the *shortest route* between two places.
   • Have the children in the class give directions to the visitor. For example, the class tells the visitor to turn left at Karen's desk or to go north at Eddie's desk.
   • Have the visitor walk silently to the friend's desk. Then have the class tell the directions the visitor traveled and the turns that he or she made. (You might want to give the children pieces of paper so they can record the directions and turns as the visitor walks.)

UNIT 4 *Making A Map of Our School*

Objective: To make and use a map of the school.
Materials: copies of Map 1 (page 108) or a map of your school; chalk (if your school has a blacktop area) or rope (if your school has a large dirt or grass area); scissors; butcher paper; stuffed animals or dolls (for Follow-Up); compass (for Follow-Up)
Vocabulary: map

LESSON 4.1   Introducing a simple school map

1. Ask the children if they know what maps are. Hand out Map 1 and explain that this is a *map* of a school. (Note: If you have a map of your school you may want to substitute it for Map 1.) Point out that each of the boxes on the map represents a classroom or office. Ask children to find various rooms on the map, for example, Room 10, the library, and the nurse's office. Point out the directions on the map. Ask the children questions such as, "Is the nurse's room north or south of the Office?" or "What is to the east of the library?"

2. Explain how maps can help us. Play a game with the children where you ask questions such as, "I am at room 3. In which direction do I have to go to get to room 4?" Continue until the children are comfortable using the map.

LESSON 4.2   Making a map of the school

1. Tell the children that today the class is going to make a map of their school. Take the class outside to a large blacktop area or a large dirt area. Make an outline of the school using the chalk or the rope (cut the rope as needed). Explain that this outline is like the boxes on the map in Lesson 4.1. (Note: If your school has two stories or is very large, you might want to map only one story or a small segment.)

2. Take the children on a trip around the school. Have them note the location of the different rooms and offices. Then return to the outline and write in the names of the rooms (if you are using the rope outline, write the room numbers and names on butcher paper, and place the paper inside the appropriate box).

3. Recheck the location of the rooms if necessary.

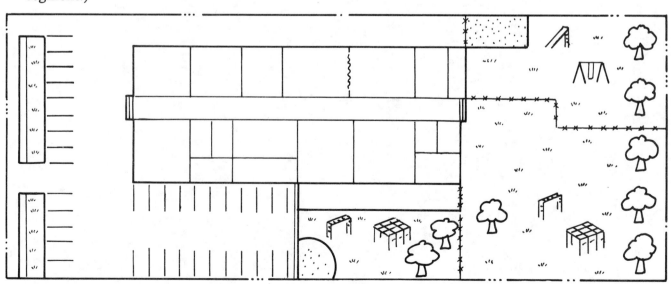

UNIT 4 continued

LESSON 4.3 Using the map of the school

1. Set up a role-playing game using the map you constructed in Lesson 4.2. Assign different children to play the principal, nurse, librarian, and various teachers from your school. Have these children stand in the map in the appropriate locations for their characters. (If the map is not large enough for the children to stand in, you should either enlarge it or have the children stand next to the "rooms.")

2. Give the remaining students simple commands, for instance, "Juanita and Jean, go to the nurse's office" or "Ray, go to Mrs. Robins's room and ask her for a book." You might also want to give the "actors" things to do.

FOLLOW-UP

1. If it is a sunny day, use the map in Lesson 4.2 to review Lesson 2.2 (page 7). Give the children simple commands such as, "Stand in Room 3. Go east one room. Where are you now?" If it is a cloudy day, you could play the same game using a compass.

2. Let the children help you redraw the map on a large sheet of butcher paper. (The redrawn map should be smaller than the original.) Take the butcher-paper map into the classroom. Play the game in Lesson 4.3, letting the children use stuffed animals or dolls to represent characters. The children can move the dolls from room to room as directed.

UNIT 5 *Making a Map of Our Classroom*

Objective: To construct a simple map of the classroom and to understand that real objects can be represented by pictures and symbols.

Materials: large sheet of butcher paper (approximately 48″ × 64″); pencil; student textbooks; compass; ½-pint milk carton for each child (for Follow-Up); photo of each child (for Follow-Up)

Vocabulary: symbol; key/legend

Lesson 5.1 Making the map

1. Review the main ideas in Unit 4 (page 11). Emphasize the importance of maps and how the class used the map they made. Tell the children that today the class will make another map—a map of the classroom.

2. Show the class the butcher paper. Ask them which is larger in size—the classroom or the paper. Explain that the paper will *represent* the classroom.

3. Draw a large rectangle to show where your desk is located. Tell the class that this rectangle is a *symbol* for your desk. Explain that most maps have symbols and a list of what the symbols mean. This list is called a *key* (or *legend*). Write *key* in the lower left hand corner of the paper. Draw a rectangle under the word and write your name next to it. Ask the children to pick a symbol to represent their desks. Write the information in the key and proceed to draw the desk symbols on the map. Have the class select a title for the map. Write the title at the top of the map. The map could look similar to Figure 6.

4. Have the children orient the map using a compass. Write the directions on the map.

5. Have the children compare the map with the classroom. Help them see that the map is selective—that it does not include everything in the room. Help the class select a title for the map. Write the title at the top of the map and place the date under it.

6. Have the children sum up the parts of a map— title, key, symbols, and so on. Then play a simulation game called "Finding My Way," where the children use the map to find their way around the classroom. (For example, you could ask a child "How many desks north is your desk from Tony's desk?")

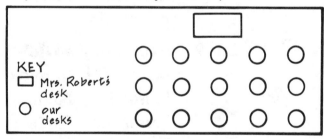

Figure 6   Sample classroom map

FOLLOW-UP

1. Make another map, this time using milk cartons to represent the desks. Help each child print his or her name on a carton. Then help the children place the cartons in the appropriate spots on the map. If you wish, children could paste pictures of themselves on the cartons.

2. Have the children go on a map hunt. Ask them to look through their textbooks for maps.

Have them identify the titles, keys, symbols, and purposes of the maps they find. You might also have them compare the purposes, symbols, orientations, and sizes of the maps.

3. Play a variation of the map hunt game. Have children look for photos, charts, or figures in the textbooks.

EXPLORING OUR ENVIRONMENT

(Suggested for Grades 2–3)

Unit 6   **Orienting Ourselves to the Environment**
Lesson 6.1   Learning the cardinal and intermediate directions
Lesson 6.2   Finding the cardinal and intermediate directions
Follow-Up

Unit 7   **Comparing Two Different Maps**
Lesson 7.1   Identifying and comparing symbols
Lesson 7.2   Identifying and comparing ways to orient yourself
Lesson 7.3   Identifying and comparing relative distances
Follow-Up

Unit 8   **Making a Map of Our Neighborhood**
Lesson 8.1   Making a semantic map
Lesson 8.2   Making a pictorial map
Follow-Up

Unit 9   **Examining a Globe of the Earth**
Lesson 9.1   Introducing globes
Lesson 9.2   Finding the cardinal directions on a globe
Lesson 9.3   Finding specific locations on a globe
Lesson 9.4   Using a globe to show night and day
Lesson 9.5   Finding circle routes on a globe
Follow-Up

Unit 10   **Comparing Maps and Globes**
Lesson 10.1   Finding the same areas on maps and globes
Lesson 10.2   Comparing keys on maps and globes
Lesson 10.3   Comparing relative distances on maps and globes
Follow-Up

UNIT 6 *Orienting Ourselves to the Environment*

Objective:	To identify and reinforce the cardinal and intermediate directions.
Materials:	yardstick or similar stick; magnetic compass; 18″ × 36″ oaktag; large marker; two large pieces of butcher paper
Vocabulary:	cardinal direction; intermediate direction; northeast; northwest; southeast; southwest

LESSON 6.1 Learning the cardinal and intermediate directions

1. Lead children through Lessons 2.2 and 2.3 (pages 7–8). Explain to the children that the four directions—north, south, east, and west—are called the *cardinal directions*.

2. Put the following information on the chalkboard:

   Intermediate Directions:
   northeast—between north and east
   northwest—between north and west
   southeast—between south and east
   southwest—between south and west

   Have the children read the information aloud. Then use a compass to show how northeast is between north and east. Explain to the children that northeast is called an *in-between* or an *intermediate* direction.

3. Draw a compass on the chalkboard or project a picture of a compass using an overhead projector. Ask the children questions such as, "Which direction is in between south and west?" Continue until the class has identified each intermediate direction.

4. On a piece of butcher paper, draw a diagram similar to the one shown in Figure 7. Have volunteers place a compass on the paper and match north on the compass with north on the diagram. Have the children identify the direction lines on the diagram by matching the lines with the corresponding lines on the compass and writing *NE, SW, S,* and so forth.

5. Have the class point out all eight directions in the classroom.

6. Repeat step 5 outside. Again, have the class point out all eight directions.

7. Review the lesson by asking questions such as "Which directions are the *cardinal* directions?" "Which directions are the *intermediate* directions?"

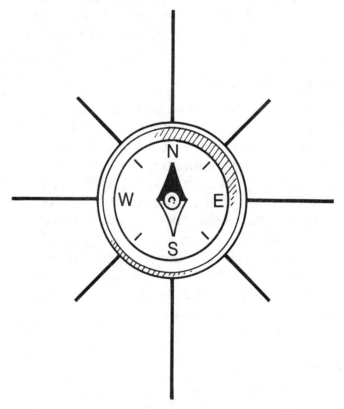

Figure 7 Using a compass to identify directions

UNIT 6 continued

LESSON 6.2   Finding the cardinal and intermediate directions

1. Review Lesson 2.2 (page 7), having the children find both the cardinal and intermediate directions.
2. Tell the children you are going to show them another way to find the directions. Take the class outside at noon. Have them stand with the sun at their backs and pick out something in front of them (for instance a flagpole or tree). Ask the children which direction they're facing (north). Then ask them the direction of their landmark from where they are standing (north). Have the children pick other landmarks for the other directions.
3. On a cloudy or foggy day, take the children outside again, and have them locate their landmarks. Ask them to point out the different directions using the landmarks. Explain that landmarks can help the children find their way.

FOLLOW-UP

1. Shortly before noon on a sunny day, take the class on a schoolyard or neighborhood walk. As the children walk, tell them which way to go using all eight directions.
2. Using all eight directions, play a "Where is It?" game. Ask the children questions such as, "I see a teacher's desk. Which direction is it from where you are sitting?" or "I see a boy with a blue- and white-striped shirt. Which direction is he from where you are sitting?" (If you play this game inside, you should post the directions on the walls.)

UNIT 7 *Comparing Two Different Maps*

Objective: To identify and compare direction, symbols, and relative distance on two maps.

Materials: transparencies and copies of Maps 2 and 3 (pages 109 and 110); ruler for each child; simple maps from textbooks (for Follow-Up)

Vocabulary: symbol; key/legend; compass rose; scale

LESSON 7.1 Identifying and comparing symbols

1. Hand out Map 2 and explain that it is a map of an imaginary or "make believe" neighborhood. Explain that each picture on the page represents a real object. For example, a small square is a *symbol* for a house. Tell the children that most maps have symbols and a list of what the symbols stand for. This list is called a *key* (or *legend*). Point out that the key helps "unlock" the meaning of the symbols.

2. Display the map using an overhead projector. Point to different symbols on the map and ask the children what each symbol represents.

3. Hand out Map 3. Ask children to find the key on the map. Then ask them to compare the symbols on Map 3 with those on Map 2. Ask questions such as, "Is the symbol for a house the same on both maps?" "Is the symbol for a school the same on both maps?" "What are some symbols on Map 3 that aren't on Map 2?" Continue until the children are comfortable with the two maps.

LESSON 7.2 Identifying and comparing ways to orient yourself

1. Review the concepts in Unit 6 (page 15). Remind children that the four main directions are called cardinal directions.

2. Display Map 2 using an overhead projector. Ask children if they know how to find directions on the map. Encourage them to make suggestions. If they need help, point out the words. Then ask the children to tell you which way north is on the map (toward the top). Have children point out the other directions.

3. Display Map 3 using the overhead projector. Ask children if they can guess how to find directions on this map. Point out the *compass rose* and explain that this symbol shows us directions. Explain that the *N* on the compass rose means north, the *S* means south, the *E* means east, and the *W* means west. Then have

the children answer questions such as, "Which way is south on Map 3?" "Which way is east on Map 3?" and so on.

4. Once children are comfortable finding the cardinal directions on the two maps, ask them how they would go about finding the intermediate directions. Point out that the intermediate directions are not written on the compass rose, but the points between the cardinal directions show the different directions. Repeat the questions from step 3, having the children find the different intermediate directions on both maps.

5. Sum up by asking the children to compare the two ways they found directions on Maps 2 and 3.

UNIT 7 continued

LESSON 7.3   Identifying and comparing relative distances

1. Review the concepts in Unit 3 (page 9). If the class needs more practice in determining distances, play "My Town" (Lesson 3.2). Refer to the distance between aisles as blocks for one game and miles for another.

2. Display Map 2. Tell the children that each large square represents one block. Have the children find the distances between different locations on the map. For instance, you might ask them questions such as, "How far is the park from house 2?" "How far is the school from the gas station?" "Give directions for the shortest route between house 1 and the school."

3. Display Map 3. Tell the children that on this map distances are measured in miles. Point to the *scale* at the bottom of the map. Explain that the scale shows how distance on the map compares with real distances. For example, on Map 3 each inch on the map is equal to one real mile. Hand out rulers and let the children find different distances on the map, such as the distance from the bridge to the intersection or the distance from house 1 to house 2.

4. Sum up the lesson by asking the children to compare the two types of distances on Map 2 and 3.

FOLLOW-UP

1. Play "Map Detective." Use Maps 2 and 3 and ask children questions such as, "The bridge is over which river?" "Is the school in Map 2 north or south of the gas station?" "Which road is the hospital next to?" (Note: If using both maps at once confuses the children, play this game using one map at a time.)

You may want to repeat the game for several days, focusing on one aspect each day—for instance, comparative distances, recognizing symbols, and finding locations.

2. Play "Map Detective" using maps from the children's textbooks.

UNIT 8 *Making a Map of Our Neighborhood*

Objective:	To make and use two maps of the neighborhood.
Materials:	yardstick or compass; scratch pads; pencils; Polaroid-type camera with film; two pieces of 24″ × 36″ newsprint or oaktag; street map of school area; first aid kit; photos of children (optional)
Vocabulary:	semantic; pictorial (both of these words are optional)

LESSON 8.1 Making a semantic map

1. Prior to starting the lesson, determine an itinerary for a field trip, including time of day, distance, and route.
2. Tell the class that today they will take a walk around the neighborhood in order to make a map. Explain that as they walk they should keep track of the following things:
   - the directions they take,
   - whose houses are along the route,
   - which stores or buildings are along the route,
   - which new buildings are being constructed (if any),
   - important landmarks such as statues, creeks, bridges, and so on.

   Pass out the pads and pencils and explain that the class will use them to sketch and list what they observe.

3. Start the walk. Have children determine directions using whatever means are available, such as the sun, shadow stick, or compass. Remind them to note distances in blocks and all changes of directions. Also remind them to note buildings and landmarks. Stop frequently to allow time for writing and sketching observations. You should take pictures of important features.

4. Once you have returned to the classroom, use the newsprint or oaktag and help the class make a semantic map similar to Figure 8. Place the school in the middle of the map and then write several important features that the children saw in each of the surrounding boxes. If the map starts to get too cluttered, make a separate map for each section (see Figure 9).

NORTH

gas station	large tree	
	school	Mary's house
	ice cream store fire station	Peter's house

WEST — EAST

SOUTH

Figure 8   Semantic map of school neighborhood

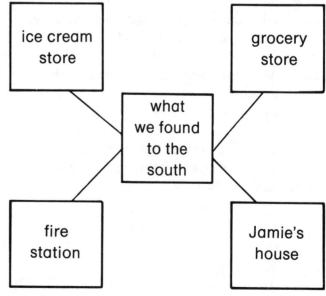

Figure 9   Expanded section of semantic map

UNIT 8 continued

LESSON 8.2   Making a pictorial map

1. Review the previous lesson. Then show the children the street map. Tell them they will make a map similar to the map you are showing them.

2. Use a street map of the school area to draw the main streets on the newsprint or oaktag. Have the children look at the semantic map and pick out common features that were found in all directions—for example, house, stores, and traffic lights. Help the children pick symbols to represent each item. Make a key on the map and record the symbols and their meanings.

3. Using the street map and the semantic map, start drawing the symbols in their appropriate locations. (If you have pictures of the children, you might want to use a child's picture to represent his or her home.) Use the pictures you took on the trip to represent features such as a fire station or a very unusual tree.

4. Help the children summarize what they did in the lessons.

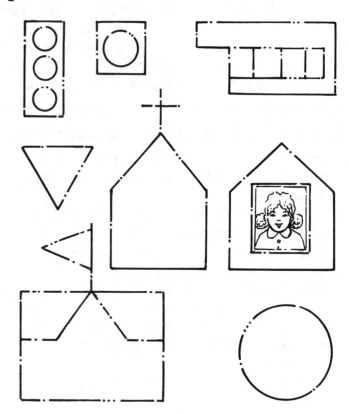

FOLLOW-UP

1. Play the "Map Detective" game from Unit 7 (page 18) using the pictorial map of the neighborhood instead of Maps 2 and 3.

2. Have the students add other symbols to the map and create route and distance questions for each other.

3. Have the students make semantic and/or pictorial maps of their neighborhoods. When making semantic maps, you may want to suggest using shapes other than squares for recording information.

UNIT 9   *Examining a Globe of the Earth*

Objective: To understand that a globe is a model of the earth and to locate specific features on a globe.

Materials: globe (large enough for class to see); pictures of the earth from space; flashlight; string or yarn; scissors

Vocabulary: globe; equator; North Pole; South Pole; rotation; circle routes

LESSON 9.1   Introducing globes

1. Show the class a large globe of the earth. Point out that a *globe* represents the earth and the shape of the globe is similar to the shape of the earth.
2. Show the children pictures of the earth from space. Ask them how the globe, the earth, and the pictures of the earth are similar. If you want, encourage children to find pictures of the earth in magazines and newspapers and use the pictures to make a bulletin-board display.

LESSON 9.2   Finding the cardinal directions on a globe

1. Review the cardinal directions.
2. Show children how to find north and south on the globe. For example, move your finger towards the North Pole and explain that you are moving north. Repeat the procedure for the south.
3. Point out the *equator*. Explain that it is a make-believe (imaginary) line around the middle of the globe that shows the east-west directions. Also explain that when you look at the North Pole, things to the right are to the east and things to the left are to the west. Be sure to emphasize that only north and south are specific points on the globe—the *North and South Poles*. Give examples of finding directions on the globe.

LESSON 9.3   Finding specific locations on a globe

1. Ask children if they know which parts of the globe show water and which show land. Point out that water is shown as blue and land is shown as other colors.
2. Point to various spots on the globe and have children identify the spot as water or land.
3. After the children are comfortable distinguishing between land and water, tell them that now they are going to find where their continent, country, and state are located. Help the children locate these places. Have them compare the sizes of the areas. Ask if there are any children who were born in different states or countries. Help these children locate their home area.

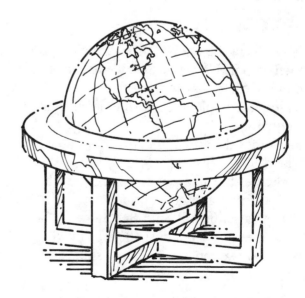

UNIT 9 continued

LESSON 9.4   Using a globe to show night and day

1. Tell the children you are going to show them how the *rotation* of the earth causes night and day.
2. Help the class find their state or the nearest city on the globe. Stick a piece of paper on the area so everyone can see it.
3. Turn the globe slowly counterclockwise so the paper goes around in a full circle. Explain that this rotation represents one day.
4. Darken the room and turn on a flashlight. Tell the children that the flashlight represents the sun. Direct the light on the paper. Ask the children whether they think it is day or night where the paper is. Turn the globe so the paper is in darkness. Ask again whether it is day or night where the paper is.
5. Explain that the sun seems to be rising and setting because the earth is turning. When we move towards the sun, it seems to rise and as we move away from the sun, it seems to set.

LESSON 9.5   Finding circle routes on a globe

1. Tell the children you are going to show them how to find distances on the globe.
2. Ask the children to suggest two places, for instance San Francisco and London. Take the piece of yarn or string and hold one end at the first point. Circle the globe with the string until you reach the second point. Then hold up the string so the children can see the stretched-out length. Tell them that the string shows the distance between the two points on the globe. If you wish, compute the actual distance using the scale found on your globe.
3. Explain that when you find distances on a globe this way, you are tracing *circle routes*. Ask the children why you can't use a straight ruler to find distances on a globe and discuss their answers.
4. Have the class take imaginary trips, for example, from Chicago to Seattle or New York to Montreal. Give children pieces of yarn and help them find the distance between the two points. You should cut off excess yarn so the children can compare the distances of different trips.

FOLLOW-UP

1. Play "Spin the Globe." Spin the globe and then stop it. Have the class identify one or more of the following:
   - the North Pole, the South Pole, and the equator
   - whether the area you point to is water or land
   - whether the area you point to is North America or another continent
2. Play a variation of "Spin the Globe." Place a small piece of paper over the area in which you live. Darken the room and shine a flashlight at the globe. Have a child spin the globe and stop it. Ask the class whether it is night or day where the paper is.
3. Have the children use the cardinal directions to tell you how to get from one place to another. For example, you might ask questions such as, "What direction do we travel to get from New York to California?" or "Is Canada north or south of the United States?" Make sure you show the locations to the children.

UNIT 10 *Comparing Maps and Globes*

Objective: To reinforce the similarities and differences between maps and globes.

Materials: globe (large enough for the class to see); wall maps of the world (large enough for the class to see); textbooks that contain pictures of different globes and maps; ruler; yarn or string; transparency or copies of Map 4 (page 111)

Vocabulary: none

LESSON 10.1 Finding the same areas on maps and globes

1. If necessary, review the concepts from Unit 7 (page 17) and Unit 9 (page 21).
2. Ask a child to find his or her home country or state on the wall map. Have the child point out the area for the class. Then ask another child to find the same area on the globe. Encourage the class to compare the two areas by asking questions such as, "Does this area have the same shape on the map and the globe?" "Is this area the same size on the map and the globe?" "Do the map and the globe show the same cities or states within the area?"
3. Play a variation of "Spin the Globe" (Follow-Up to Unit 9). Spin the globe and stop it. Have the class find the area you are pointing to on the wall map.

LESSON 10.2 Comparing keys on maps and globes

1. Have the children find the key on the wall map. Discuss some of the symbols in the key. Then have the class find the key on the globe. Ask the class to compare the keys. Ask questions such as, "Are the symbols the same?" "What are some symbols on the wall map that don't appear on the globe?" "What are some symbols on the globe that don't appear on the wall map?"
2. Have the children look at different maps in textbooks. Compare the symbols on the maps with those on the wall map and the globe.

LESSON 10.3 Comparing relative distances on maps and globes

1. Have the children pick two points on the wall map. Using a piece of string or a ruler, compute the distance between the two points. Then find the distance between the two points on the globe. Again, compute the real distance between the two points.
2. Ask children to compare the ways you found the distance on the map and the globe. Point out that you can't use a ruler to measure distances on the globe.
3. Help children find the distances between other points on the map and the globe. Then have them look at pictures of different maps in textbooks. Have them compare the scale and distances of these maps with those on the wall map and the globe.

FOLLOW-UP

1. Have the children go on a map and globe hunt. Encourage them to find one particular area on different maps and globes. You could also ask them to find the distance between two points on different maps and globes.
2. Display or hand out Map 4. Have children compare Maps A and B.

GOING BEYOND OUR ENVIRONMENT

(Suggested for Grades 3–4)

Unit 11 Comparing Maps and Photos
     Lesson 11.1   Being a photo detective
     Lesson 11.2   Comparing a map with a photo
     Follow–Up

Unit 12 Comparing Road Maps
     Lesson 12.1   Introducing road maps
     Lesson 12.2   Finding locations on road maps
     Lesson 12.3   Finding distances on road maps
     Follow–Up

Unit 13 Determining Size and Shape
     Lesson 13.1   Comparing the scale of two maps
     Lesson 13.2   Estimating the areas of different places
     Follow–Up

Unit 14 Introducing Height and Elevation
     Lesson 14.1   Using a triangle to determine height
     Lesson 14.2   Using symbols to show elevation
     Follow–Up

Unit 15 Making a Relief Map
     Lesson 15.1   Introducing relief maps
     Lesson 15.2   Making the relief map
     Follow–Up

UNIT 11 *Comparing Maps and Photos*

Objective: To recognize that maps and photos can show the same areas.
Materials: transparency and copies of Map 5 (page 112); transparencies of Photos 1 and 2 (pages 135 and 136); photos from social studies textbooks (for Follow-Up)
Vocabulary: none

LESSON 11.1   Being a photo detective

1. Tell the class that they are going to play a game called "Photo Detective." Explain that you are going to display a photo and the class will have to look at the photo and remember as much about it as they can. Tell the students that they will have only 15 seconds to look at the photo. Once the projector is turned off, students should list or sketch everything they saw in the photo. (Students should not be concerned about spelling or artwork.)
2. Project Photo 1A for 15 seconds. Allow the students two minutes to work on their lists or sketches. Then tell the class to stop.
3. Ask students to write a good title for the photo.
4. Project the photo again to check the recorded data. If you wish, you can incorporate a point system. Give two points for every correct observation and title, regardless of spelling or drawing quality. Subtract one point for any items listed or sketched that are not in the photo.
5. Repeat steps 2–4 using Photo 1B.
6. If you want, repeat steps 2–4 using photos from students' textbooks.

LESSON 11.2   Comparing a map with a photo

1. Distribute Map 5 to students. Display Photos 1A and 2. Ask the class to tell you which photo has been mapped. Discuss the reasons for their answers.
2. Place the transparency of Map 5 over Photo 2 so students can match various shapes and phenomena in the photo with the map.
3. Discuss the symbols used on the map. Point out that some of the items that appear in the photo don't appear on the map. Ask students to find examples of things which appear in the photo and not on the map. Then ask them what symbols could be used to represent the missing items. Have the students add some of the symbols to their maps while you add them to the transparency. Make sure the students also add the symbols to the map key.
4. Ask the class to pick a title for the map. List choices on the chalkboard and help the class determine the most appropriate title. Have the students write the title on their maps.
5. Discuss how the map is different from the photo. Encourage responses such as the following:
   - A symbol on a map represents something, while a photo is a picture of it.
   - We can use any type of symbol to represent something on a map. A photo shows only the actual objects.
   - A photo includes everything the photographer and camera lens take in, while a map includes only what the map maker puts in. Therefore, a map may not show everything that the photo shows.

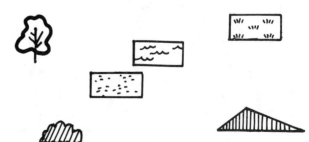

UNIT 11 continued

FOLLOW-UP

1. Have the students go outside in pairs or small groups, select a direction, observe the area for 15 seconds, turn away, and record their observations.
2. Repeat Follow-Up 1. After the students have recorded their observations, have them draw a semantic map of what they saw. When they are finished, let them check their maps against the area they observed.
3. Display a photo from a textbook. Have the class make a map of the photo. Help the class choose a title for their maps.
4. Display or project any photo you have used, and play "Examples and Nonexamples" game using "Photo Detective" procedures from Lesson 11.1. This time have children fold paper in half with an E at the top of one column and an N at the top of the other. Have the class note all examples of buildings, for instance under E. Then reshow photo and have them record nonexamples in the other column.

UNIT 12 *Comparing Road Maps*

Objective:	To draw conclusions about locations using road maps.
Materials:	transparency and copies of Map 6 (page 113); transparencies of Figures 10 and 11 (page 29); ruler for each student; transparency of a road map (for Follow-Up); copies of hometown road maps (for Follow-Up)
Vocabulary:	interstate highway; mileage table; road map; state highway; U.S. highway

LESSON 12.1   Introducing road maps

1. Hand out copies of Map 6. Explain that Maps 6A and 6B are called road maps. Point out that road maps show us how to get from one place to another.
2. Tell students to look at Map 6A. Review previously learned map skills by asking questions such as, "What is the title of Map 6A?" "How can we find directions on this map?" "What symbols are shown in the key?" Repeat for Map 6B.
3. Ask students how the two maps are similar—for example, they both show major roads of the areas, and they both show *state highways, U.S. highways,* and *interstate highways.* Then ask students how the maps are different.
4. Have students go on a map hunt. Ask them to find road maps in their textbooks. Sum up the lesson by asking students to explain why this type of map is called a *road map.*

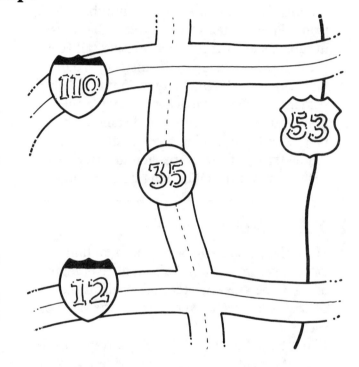

LESSON 12.2   Finding locations on road maps

1. Project Map 6A. Ask students to find and orient different locations on the map. For example, you might ask, "What direction would you go to get from Chad to Alta?" "Is Elton north or south of Boyd?" "What two highways connect Chad and Elton?" "What interstate highways would you take to get from Alta to Denny?"
2. Place the transparency of Figure 10 over Map 6A. Explain that this grid helps people find locations more easily. Point out the letters that name the spaces from top to bottom and the numbers that name the spaces from side to side. Tell the class that the location of

any place on the map can be described by putting a letter and a number together. For example, Boyd is located in space C-3. Count down to space C and across to space 3 to show the students how to locate the space.
3. Call out grid spaces on the map, for example, B-1, C-5, and D-5. Ask students to tell you the places located in those squares. Then name places and ask the students to tell you which squares they are located in.
4. Repeat steps 1-3 using Map 6B.
5. Review the concepts of finding locations on road maps.

UNIT 12 continued

LESSON 12.3   Finding distances on road maps

1. Project Map 6A. Ask students what the scale of the map is. Review how the scale shows how distances on the map compare with real distances. Hand out rulers and have the class find distances *along the roads* between cities.
2. Now project Map 6B. Ask what the scale of the map is. Then point out the numbers printed next to the roads. Explain that these numbers show the number of miles between the cities. For example, the distance from Gardenville to Dream City is 25 miles. Ask students to check the distance using a ruler.
3. Have students find different distances on the map. Ask the following types of questions: "How far is it from Fairgarten to After?" "How far is it from Gardenville to Before?" "Is it shorter to go from Dream City to After by way of Before or by way of Gardenville?" "What is the shortest route from Before to Fairgarten?" "How long is Highway 41 between Gardenville and Champion?"
4. Project Figure 11. Explain that this chart is called a *mileage table*. A mileage table can help people find distances between larger cities. Show the class how to use the table. Look for the city you are starting from on the left side of the table. Then, at the top of the table, look for the city you are going to. The distance between the two cities is shown where the lines for the two cities meet. Ask the students to find distance between different cities using the chart.

FOLLOW-UP

1. Have the children go on a road-map hunt. Encourage them to find different road maps of the same area. Ask them to check if the distances between two points are the same on each map.
2. Play "How Far Is It?" Display a transparency of a road map. Ask the class to pick two points on the map and find the distance between them.
3. Ask the children to calculate the distances between places on a map of their hometown or state. Have them make a mileage table to show the different distances.

Figure 10   A map grid

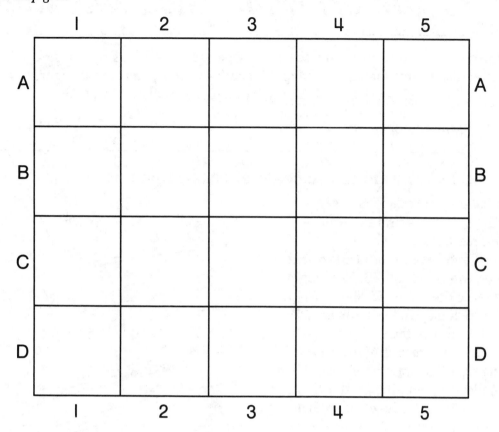

Figure 11   Mileage table for Map 6B

	After	Before	Champion	Dream City	Early	Fairgarten	Gardenville
After		40	90	60	100	85	35
Before	40		65	35	75	100	50
Champion	90	65		30	70	105	55
Dream City	60	35	30		40	75	25
Early	100	75	70	40		45	65
Fairgarten	85	100	105	75	45		50
Gardenville	35	50	55	25	65	50	

UNIT 13 *Determining Size and Shape*

Objective: To compare the size and shape of land areas using maps.
Materials: transparency of Map 7 (page 114); transparencies of Figures 12–15 (pages 31–32); world map (for Follow-Up); social studies textbooks (for Follow-Up)
Vocabulary: area

LESSON 13.1   Comparing the scale of two maps

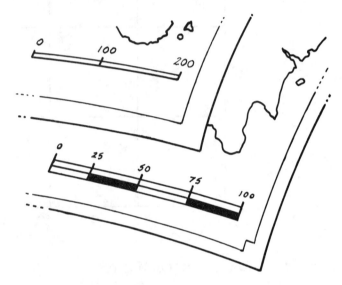

1. Review the concept of scale from Lesson 7.3 (page 18). Have students find the scale on maps in their textbooks.
2. Project Map 7 and have the students orient themselves on Maps 7A and 7B. You might ask, "What place does Map 7A show? Map 7B?" and "Which map shows more *area*?"
3. Have students compare the scale on both maps. Ask students if they can make a statement relating scale and amount of area shown. (The more miles per inch, the greater the area shown.) Also ask students how a map that shows a greater area (Map 7B) would be useful and how a map that shows less area (Map 7A) would be useful.

LESSON 13.2   Estimating the areas of different places

1. Project Figure 12. Discuss the shape of each state. Have the class identify the two states that extend a greater distance from east-west than from north to south. Also have them name the two states that extend a greater distance from north-south.
2. Next, have the students compare the size of the states. Ask them to rank the states from largest in area to smallest in area. Write their estimates on the chalkboard. Tape a piece of paper over the writing.
3. Project Figure 13, which shows the actual areas of the states. Have children rank the areas and then uncover their original estimates. If there are any differences between the two lists, discuss the reasons why the students guessed as they did.
4. Repeat the exercise using Figures 14 and 15.

FOLLOW-UP

1. Have students search for different scaled maps of the same area in their textbooks. Ask them to keep a record of the maps and their scales.
2. Display a world map. Ask the class to find countries that are similar in shape even if they are not similar in size (for example, India and Brazil; and Australia and China).
3. Use a globe or a world map to make cutout shapes of different countries. Place the cutouts on an overhead projector and ask the students to compare the shapes and sizes of the places. Have them check their size comparisons in a social studies textbook, encyclopedia, or almanac.

Figure 12   Outlines of four western states

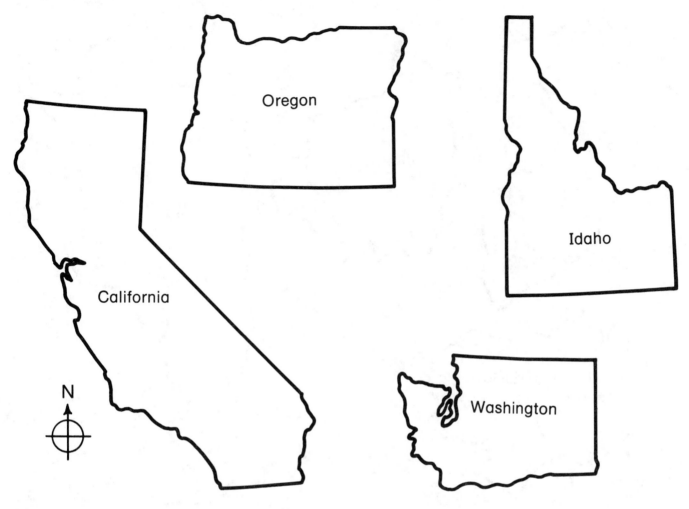

Figure 13   Table showing areas of four western states

TABLE I   AREAS OF FOUR WESTERN STATES

State	Area (in sq. miles)
California	158,693
Idaho	83,557
Oregon	96,981
Washington	68,192

Figure 14   Outline of four South American countries

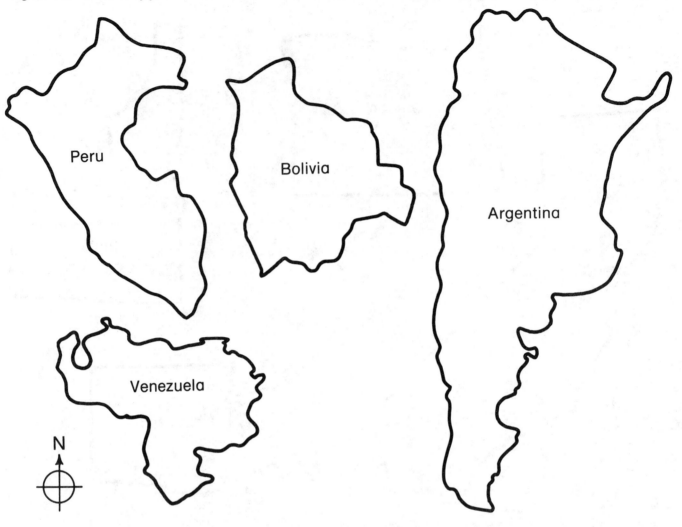

Figure 15   Table showing areas of four South American countries

TABLE 2   AREAS OF FOUR SOUTH AMERICAN COUNTRIES

Country	Area (in sq. miles)
Argentina	1,072,889
Bolivia	424,165
Peru	496,225
Venezuela	352,145

UNIT 14 *Introducing Height and Elevation*

Objective: To identify the four basic landforms using a physical map and a cross-section diagram.

Materials: transparencies of Maps 8 and 9 (pages 115–116); right triangles cut from tagboard (see Figure 16 for dimensions—there should be one triangle for each group of four students); social studies textbooks; clay (for Follow-Up)

Vocabulary: cross section; landform; plateau; physical map; elevation

LESSON 14.1   Using a triangle to determine height

1. Review the concepts from Unit 13 (page 30). Explain that today the class will explore the height of objects.

2. Show the class one of the cutout triangles. Point out the right angle (see Figure 16). Explain that the class will be using these triangles to measure the heights of different things.

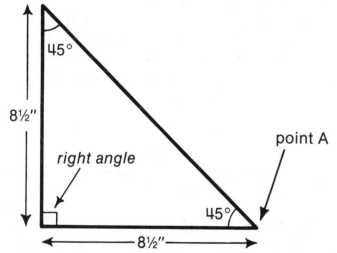

Figure 16   Triangle used to find heights of objects

3. Divide the class into groups of four and give one child in each group a triangle. Take the children outside and find a fairly tall tree. Show the class how to hold the triangle—with point A at eye level and the base of the triangle parallel to the ground. Point the triangle at the tree and move backward or forward until you can see the top of the tree along an imaginary line from point A of the triangle to the top of the tree. (See Figure 17.)

4. Explain that to find the height of the tree, you have to count the number of feet (in this activity one giant step equals one foot) from the person holding the triangle to the base of the tree. Then you add the number of feet to the tree to the height of the person holding the triangle. This number will be the approximate height of the tree. For example, if you are ten giant steps from the tree and you are six feet tall, the tree would be ten feet plus six feet high, or sixteen feet high.

5. Have one person in each group align the triangle with the top of the tree. Then have another person count the number of giant steps from the first person to the tree. After the first two children are done, have the other two children in each group repeat the measurement.

6. Once the students have finished measuring the height of the tree, have them measure other objects in the area, such as buildings, flagpoles, and telephone poles until they are comfortable finding the heights of objects.

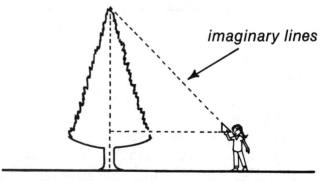

Figure 17   Finding the heights of objects

UNIT 14 continued

LESSON 14.2   Using symbols to show elevation

1. Draw Figure 18 on the chalkboard. Explain that this drawing shows a *cross section* of the height (from sea level) or *elevation* of South America. Explain that a cross section of the land shows us the earth as if we could cut into it and see a slice of it. Ask students how this type of picture could help us find the high and low spots of South America.

2. Use the diagram to introduce the four basic landforms to the class. Ask questions such as, "Which letters indicate the highest elevations or the mountains?" (A and E) "Which letter shows the lowest elevation or the plains?" (C) "Which letter shows us hills, which look like smaller rounded mountains?" (B) "Where do we see plateaus, which are high and level?" (D).

3. Display Map 8. Ask the students which two types of landforms are shown on this map. (Mountains and plains.) Point out each type on the map. Ask the class which symbol indi-

cates the highest elevations. (The symbol for mountains.)

4. Display Map 9. Ask the children to point out the differences between Map 8 and Map 9. (The symbols for mountains are different.) Explain that there are several different ways to show elevation. Two of these ways are to use "pictorial" symbols, as in Map 8, and lines, dots, or shading, as in Map 9. Explain that maps that show landforms and elevation are called *physical maps*. Physical maps show us the physical features of the land.

5. Have students look in their textbooks to find other physical maps that use symbols to indicate elevation. Ask them to point out some of the other features that physical maps show, such as rivers and lakes.

6. Review the terms and elevation concepts as needed to help students understand that symbols on maps are a way to show elevation.

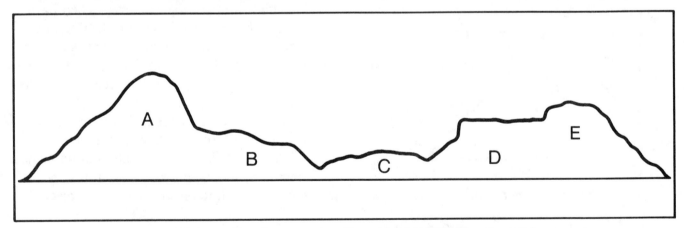

Figure 18   Cross section diagram of South America

FOLLOW-UP

1. Take the class outside and have them record the heights of different objects. They should use a triangle to find the heights. Then return to the classroom and have the students sketch what they saw, using different colors or symbols to indicate the different heights.

2. Hand out clay to pairs of students. Have them reconstruct each elevation from Figure 18. Then have them label each landform.

UNIT 15 *Making a Relief Map*

Objective: To construct a simple relief map from a physical map.
Materials: transparency of Map 8 or Map 9 (pages 115–116); transparency of a simple physical map; relief map showing western United States; small box covered with shelf paper and filled with sand, or clay and cardboard or wood board; copies of simple physical maps (for Follow-Up)
Vocabulary: physical map; relief map

LESSON 15.1   Introducing relief maps

1. If necessary, review the concepts from Lesson 14.2 (page 34).
2. Display Map 8 or Map 9. Ask students to point out the different landforms. Then show the class a relief map of the same area. Point out that the *relief map* is raised in the places where the *physical map* shows mountains and low in the places where the physical map shows plains. Ask the class why they think relief maps might be useful.
3. Have the class find other similarities and differences in the two maps.

LESSON 15.2   Making the relief map

1. Explain that today the class will make a relief map. Place the clay and board (or box filled with sand) on a cleared-off table. Project a simple physical map.
2. Tell the class that you will mold the clay or sand to show the same physical features that are on the physical map. If you are using clay, flatten out the clay into the basic outline of the map you are using. Then mold elevated mountains out of clay and place them on their approximate locations on the map outline. If you are using sand, wet the sand slightly.

Draw an outline of the area, and scoop out sand to form plains and mountains. (You might have several children help you make the map.)

3. Once the map is finished, have the class select a title for the map and make a key. Then have the class compare the finished relief map with the projected physical map. Discuss why certain areas may have been accented more or less on the relief map. Help the class understand that mapmakers are selective—different mapmakers will include different information.

FOLLOW-UP

1. Have the class make a simple physical map of a small area outside. Then supply the students with clay and have them make a relief map of the same area.
2. Hand out copies of a simple physical map. Have the students use clay to make a relief map of the area.
3. Hand out copies of a simple physical map. Have students choose colors for the different elevations and color the map. Make sure they note the color choices in the key.

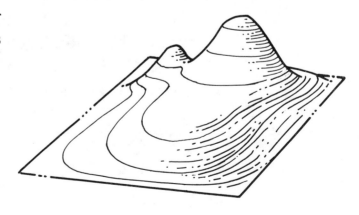

DISCOVERING OUR REGION AND NATION

(Suggested for Grades 4–5)

Unit 16 Examining Maps of the United States
Lesson 16.1   Interpreting a political map
Lesson 16.2   Interpreting a regional map
Follow-Up

Unit 17 Comparing Different Ways to Show Scale
Lesson 17.1   Comparing statement of scale and graphic scale
Lesson 17.2   Using scale to determine distance
Follow-Up

Unit 18 Exploring United States Time Zones
Lesson 18.1   Introducing time zones
Lesson 18.2   Using a time zone map
Follow-Up

Unit 19 Exploring Elevation
Lesson 19.1   Recognizing landforms on cross section diagrams
Lesson 19.2   Recognizing landforms on shaded or colored maps
Follow-Up

Unit 20 Using Distribution Maps
Lesson 20.1   Reading and using a population map
Lesson 20.2   Reading and using a product map
Lesson 20.3   Reading and using a precipitation map
Lesson 20.4   Gathering information from different distribution maps
Follow-Up

UNIT 16 *Examining Maps of the United States*

Objective: To use previously learned skills to gather information from a U.S. map.

Materials: transparencies of Maps 4A, 10, and 11 (pages 111 and 117-118); atlas, encyclopedia or social studies textbook; 8½″ × 11″ blank transparency (for Follow-Up); copies of Maps 10 and 11 (for Follow-Up)

Vocabulary: outline map; political map; political boundaries; natural boundaries; state boundary; international boundary; regions; the West; the South; the Northeast; and the Midwest

LESSON 16.1 Interpreting a political map

1. Project Map 4A. Point out that this map is an *outline map* of North America. Ask the class why this type of map might be called an outline map. (It only shows the outline of North America.) Now project Map 10. Have students compare this map with Map 4A. Help them discover that Map 10 shows boundaries between the countries and states.

2. Explain that most of the boundaries between the countries and states are not necessarily real boundaries, since people decide where the boundaries will be. These types of boundaries are called *political boundaries*. Show the class some of the political boundaries. Maps that show political boundaries are called *political maps*. Also point out that some boundary lines follow natural features of the land, such as rivers, oceans, and lakes. This type of boundary is

called a *natural boundary*. Ask the class to tell you some of the natural boundaries.

3. Point to different boundary lines on the map and ask students if the lines are natural boundaries or political boundaries. Also ask students how they can tell the difference between an *international boundary* (a boundary between countries) and a *state boundary*. (The symbols are different.)

4. Play a "Map Detective" game with the students. Ask them questions about the map. For example, "What is the natural boundary on the East Coast of the United States?" "What states or countries border our home state?" "Which state in the United States reaches the farthest south?" "How many different states border Utah?" "What river makes a border on the west side of Iowa?" Continue until the students are comfortable finding locations on the map.

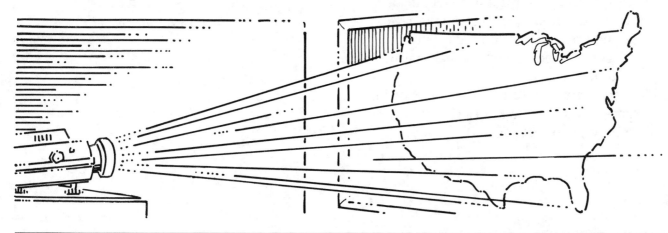

UNIT 16 continued

LESSON 16.2   Interpreting a regional map

1. Project Map 10 and then project Map 11. Ask students to tell you what other boundaries have been added to Map 11. Point out that the boundaries on Map 11 divide the United States into parts or *regions*. The regions shown on Map 11 are the West, the South, the Midwest, and the Northeast. Have students match each regional name with the correct area on the map. Then ask students which region their state is in.

2. Point to the state abbreviations on the map. Ask students if they recognize these abbreviations. If they do not, help them realize that these are the abbreviations used by the post office. Have students tell you the names of some of the states.

3. Play the "Map Detective" game from Lesson 16.1. You might ask questions such as, "Which region contains the greatest number of states?" "Which region contains the least number of states?" "Name three states located in the West." "Which region has a natural boundary on the west?" "What is that boundary?"

4. Have students compare the sizes of the regions. You should have them try to rank the regions from greatest area to least area. Then have them use an atlas, encyclopedia, or social studies textbooks to check their answers.

FOLLOW-UP

1. Make a transparency of a grid similar to the one shown in Figure 19. The grid should be the same size as Map 10. Place the grid over the transparency of Map 10. Have students identify different locations using the names of the grid squares. (Note: If necessary, use Lesson 12.2 [page 27] to review the use of grids.)

2. Hand out copies of Maps 10 and 11. Have children locate a physical map of the United States in a textbook. Ask them to compare the elevations and features of different states and regions. For instance, you might have them find the regions that have mostly mountains and the regions that have mostly plains or lowlands.

3. Have students locate other political maps in textbooks. Ask them to keep a record of the different types of boundaries they find.

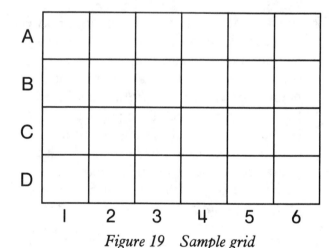

Figure 19   Sample grid

UNIT 17 *Comparing Different Ways to Show Scale*

Objective: To determine relative distances using statement of scale and graphic scale.

Materials: copies of Maps 7 and 13 (pages 114 and 120); transparency of Map 12 (page 119); rulers; 3″ × 5″ blank transparency; copies of Group Activity A (pages 41–42); social studies textbooks (for Follow-Up)

Vocabulary: statement of scale; graphic scale; ratio (optional)

LESSON 17.1   Comparing statement of scale and graphic scale

1. Use Lesson 13.1 (page 30) to review the concept of scale. Point out that the scales shown on Map 7 are only one way to show scale. Explain that on Map 7A, the scale is shown with words—for example, 1 inch = 100 miles. When scale is written this way it is called *statement of scale*. We just say or write the scale like a sentence.

2. Hand out copies of Map 7 and rulers. Have students find distances between places on Map 7A. For example, you might ask them to find the distance between Albany and Macon, Atlanta and Savannah, and Athens and Valdosta. Remind the class that they should tell you the distances in terms of miles, not inches.

3. Project Map 12. Ask students to point out the scale on this map. (Bottom lefthand corner.) Have the students tell you how this way to show scale is different than using statement of scale. (This type of scale only shows a line and numbers.) Tell students that this type of scale is called a *graphic scale*. Explain that on this map, the length of the line from the 0 to the 25 equals twenty-five miles, and the length of the line from the 0 to the 50 equals fifty miles.

4. Show students how to find distances using a graphic scale. Explain that with this type of scale, you don't need to use a ruler. Take the 3″ × 5″ blank transparency and lay it along one of the highways shown on Map 12. (The road from Ft. Dodge to Cedar Falls works well as an example.) Trace a straight line along the road, marking a point when you need to move the card because of a curve or bend. (See Figure 20.) When you are finished, put the card next to the scale and

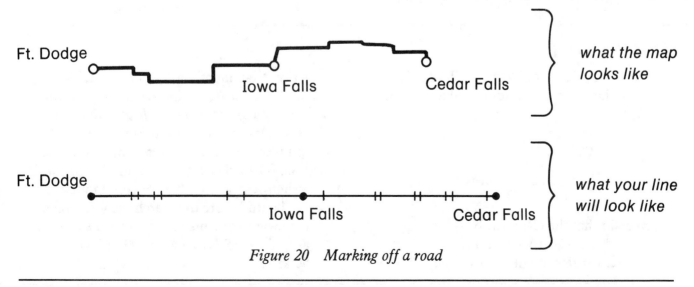

Figure 20   Marking off a road

mark off the distance on your "road" line. (See Figure 21.) Then compute the distance of the path. (For example, the distance between Ft. Dodge and Cedar Falls would be approximately 110 miles.)

5. Compute the distances between several other places, so students understand how it is done. You might have the students guide you by telling you when to turn the card and by counting off the number of miles.

6. Have students look through their social studies textbooks to find maps with and without scales. Have them explain, on paper, how to tell distance on each map.

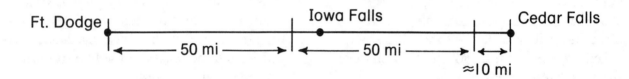

Figure 21   Finding the distance of a road

LESSON 17.2   Using scale to determine distance

1. Distribute Map 13 and Group Activity A to the students. Read the directions aloud, emphasizing that students have to use differ-ent types of scale for different parts of the activity. You may want to do the activity aloud with students who have difficulty with it.

FOLLOW-UP

1. Play a "Scale Hunt" game. Tell the class to write the following headings on a piece of paper:

> **Page**
> **Map Title**
> **Way Scale is Shown**
> **Scale**

Explain that the class will be searching through their textbooks to find maps with different scales. Point out that they should write "statement" or "graphic" under *Way Scale is Shown* and the actual scale (i.e., 1 inch = 70 miles) under the *Scale* column. Allow the class a specific amount of time, such as three minutes, to conduct their hunt. When the time is up, check their findings. If you wish, write the page numbers of certain maps on the board before the search begins. You also may want students to look for scales shown as *ratios* (such as 1 inch : 300 miles or ½ in. : 50 km).

Group Activity A Using Scale To Determine Distance

Use Map 13. Circle the letter of the numeral or phrase that best answers each question. Use either the statement of scale or the graphic scale to answer questions 1–5; use the statement of scale to answer questions 6–10; use the graphic scale to answer questions 11–15.

1. If you drive from Jackson to Indio and then on to Happydale, how many miles will you travel?
   a. 15   c. 35
   b. 25   d. 45

2. If you returned to Jackson from Happydale by traveling southeast on the highway and then turning right on Route 1, how far would you have to drive?
   a. 15 miles   c. 35 miles
   b. 25 miles   d. 40 miles

3. If you go south from Jackson, what is the approximate number of miles between Jackson and Lolo?
   a. 15   c. 35
   b. 25   d. 45

4. How far is it from Kelso to Manjo?
   a. 5 miles   c. 15 miles
   b. 10 miles   d. 20 miles

5. If you drive from Happydale to Barton, approximately how far have you gone?
   a. 12 miles   c. 22 miles
   b. 17 miles   d. 27 miles

6. What is the number of miles between Apple Valley and Barton?
   a. 20   c. 30
   b. 25   d. 35

7. The *shortest* route from Apple Valley to Indio would be about _____ miles.
   a. 32   c. 58
   b. 48   d. 72

8. If you returned to Apple Valley from Indio, driving through Happydale and Barton, about how many miles would you travel?
   a. 32   c. 58
   b. 48   d. 72

9. Route 1 is about _____ miles long.
   a. 27   c. 42
   b. 37   d. 47

10. If you drove south from Jackson, turned left on Manjo Road, and drove to Manjo, approximately how many miles would you drive?
    a. 20   c. 40
    b. 30   d. 55

11. If you drove on Route 1 from Jackson, turned right on the highway, and drove to Manjo, approximately how many miles would you drive?
    a. 35   c. 45
    b. 40   d. 50

12. If you go north on the highway, it is _____ miles between Lolo and Indio.
    a. 25   c. 35
    b. 30   d. 40

13. Driving northwest, approximately how far is it from Manjo to Route 1?
    a. 10 miles   c. 20 miles
    b. 14 miles   d. 27 miles

14. If you drive from Happydale to Manjo, traveling southeast on the highway, how many miles would you travel?
    a. 10   c. 25
    b. 20   d. 35

15. If you go from Lolo, stopping in Jackson and Indio, it is _____ miles to Happydale.
    a. 25   c. 30
    b. 28   d. 40

UNIT 18 *Exploring United States Time Zones*

Objective: To read and use a time zone map of the United States.
Materials: transparency and copies of Map 14 (page 121); wall map of the United States; copies of Group Activity B (page 44)
Vocabulary: time zone; daylight savings time (optional)

LESSON 18.1 Introducing time zones

1. If necessary, use Lesson 16.1 (page 37) to review the concept of boundaries. Point out that Map 10 shows the boundaries between states and countries, and Map 11 shows the boundaries between states and regions.
2. Display Map 14. Explain that this map shows another type of boundary. Ask the students to use the key to find what the new boundary is (*time zone* boundaries). Explain that the earth is constantly changing its orientation in relation to the sun. As the earth moves, the sun appears to move from east to west across the United States. Therefore, it can be dark in New York while it is still light in California.
3. Pull down a wall map of the United States so students can see the actual positions of Alaska and Hawaii. Ask students how many time zones the continental United States is divided into (4), and then ask how many time zones the whole United States is divided into (7). Make sure you point out that time zone boundaries are not the same as state boundaries— one part of a state may be in one time zone while another part is in another time zone.
4. Point to different states on the map and ask students to tell you which time zone the state is in. Also ask them to name some of the states that are in more than one time zone.

LESSON 18.2 Using a time zone map

1. Distribute copies of Map 14 and Group Activity B to each pair of students. Read the directions aloud. Have each pair write their names on the papers.
2. Do several sample questions before beginning the activity. For example, you might ask, "What is the difference in time between Virginia and Nevada?" "What time zone is our state in?" "If it were 10:00 A.M. in Texas, what time would it be in Florida?" "In Iowa?"
3. Have students do the activity. You might want to do the activity aloud with students who have difficulty with it. When all the students are finished, have pairs of students report their answers aloud to the class.

FOLLOW-UP

1. Have a discussion with the class about daylight savings time.
2. Play "Tell Me the Time." Divide the class into four groups. Call one group *Pacific Standard Time*, one *Mountain Standard Time*, one *Central Standard Time*, and one *Eastern Standard Time*. Tell the class that you are going to make a statement such as, "It is 12:00 P.M. Eastern Standard Time," and then you will point to a group and ask them what time it is in their time zone. If they give the correct answer, they get to choose the next time. For example, you might say, "It is 10:00 P.M. Mountain Standard Time," and point to the Pacific Standard Time group. They answer correctly with "It is 9:00 P.M." Then they call out, "It is 2:30 A.M. Pacific Standard Time," and point to another group.

Group Activity B   Working with Time

Use Map 14. Circle the letter of the word or numeral that best answers each question.

1. Hawaii Standard Time is the same as _____ Standard Time.
   a. Alaska   c. Pacific
   b. Bering   d. Yukon

2. What time zone is Nevada in?
   a. Yukon   c. Pacific
   b. Mountain   d. Central

3. What time zone is Washington in?
   a. Pacific   c. Central
   b. Mountain   d. Eastern

4. Iowa is in the same time zone as _____ .
   a. Oregon   c. Virginia
   b. Arizona   d. Missouri

5. What time zone is Georgia in?
   a. Hawaii   c. Mountain
   b. Eastern   d. Pacific

6. New Mexico and Utah are both located in the _____ Time Zone.
   a. Alaska   c. Central
   b. Yukon   d. Mountain

7. Oklahoma is located in the _____ Time Zone.
   a. Alaska   c. Central
   b. Yukon   d. Mountain

8. Colorado is divided into _____ time zones.
   a. 1   c. 3
   b. 2   d. 4

9. Indiana is divided into _____ time zones.
   a. 1   c. 3
   b. 2   d. 4

10. South Dakota is divided into _____ time zones.
    a. 1   c. 3
    b. 2   d. 4

Group Activity B continued

11. Alabama is divided into _____ time zones.
    - a. 1
    - b. 2
    - c. 3
    - d. 4

12. Alaska is divided into _____ time zones.
    - a. 1
    - b. 2
    - c. 3
    - d. 4

13. How many hours difference is there between Iowa and Oregon?
    - a. 1
    - b. 2
    - c. 3
    - d. 4

14. How many hours difference is there between Virginia and California?
    - a. 0
    - b. 2
    - c. 3
    - d. 5

15. How many hours difference is there between Utah and Ohio?
    - a. 0
    - b. 2
    - c. 3
    - d. 5

16. How many hours difference is there between New York and most of Florida?
    - a. 0
    - b. 2
    - c. 3
    - d. 5

17. If it is 4:00 A.M. in most of Kansas, what time is it in South Carolina?
    - a. 2:00 A.M.
    - b. 3:00 A.M.
    - c. 4:00 A.M.
    - d. 5:00 A.M.

18. If it is 12:00 P.M. in Hawaii, what time is it in Maine?
    - a. 2:00 P.M.
    - b. 3:00 P.M.
    - c. 4:00 P.M.
    - d. 5:00 P.M.

19. If it is 3:00 A.M. in Mississippi, what time is it in Oregon?
    - a. 1:00 A.M.
    - b. 2:00 A.M.
    - c. 3:00 A.M.
    - d. 4:00 A.M.

20. If it is 7:00 P.M. in New Jersey, what time is it in Wisconsin?
    - a. 5:00 P.M.
    - b. 6:00 P.M.
    - c. 7:00 P.M.
    - d. 8:00 P.M.

UNIT 19 *Exploring Elevation*

Objective: To identify landforms on shaded and colored physical maps.
Materials: transparencies of Maps 8 and 15 (pages 115 and 122); social studies textbooks; tracing paper or blank transparencies for each student (for Follow-Up); copies of Map 8 (for Follow-Up)
Vocabulary: landform; cross section

LESSON 19.1 Recognizing landforms on cross section diagrams

1. Use Lesson 14.2 (page 34) to review the concepts of landforms and cross section diagrams. Draw Figure 22 on the chalkboard. Read the title and descriptions aloud. Explain that the task is to find which elevation (A–F) best fits each word description (1–4).

2. As a group, match the elevations with the word descriptions. Then read the correct answers aloud and have students check their own work. (Answers: A-1; B-3; C-4; D-1; E-2; F-1)

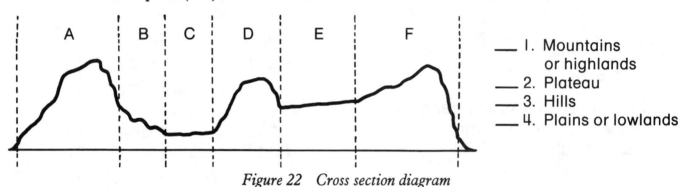

Figure 22 Cross section diagram

__ 1. Mountains or highlands
__ 2. Plateau
__ 3. Hills
__ 4. Plains or lowlands

LESSON 19.2 Recognizing landforms on shaded or colored maps

1. Project Map 8. Ask the students which two types of landforms are shown on this map (mountains and plains). Point out each type on the map. Then project Map 15. Ask students what other landform appears on Map 15 (*plateaus*). Point out that the different landforms are shown with shading.

2. Have the class look through their textbooks to find colored physical maps. Point out that the colored maps can show the different elevations and landforms more clearly.

3. Sum up the lesson by reviewing the different ways that students have learned to show elevation—cross sections, symbols, shading, and color.

FOLLOW-UP

1. Have students look for cross section diagrams in social studies and science textbooks. Ask them to make a list showing the page number, title, and type of diagram.

2. Hand out tracing paper or clear transparencies to students. Have them locate side-

view pictures of mountains and trace the elevation to produce a cross section.

3. Hand out copies of Map 8. Have students make cross section diagrams of the map.

UNIT 20 *Using Distribution Maps*

Objective: To read and use different types of distribution maps.
Materials: transparencies of Maps 11 and 16–19 (pages 118 and 123–126); copies of Maps 17 and 18; social studies textbooks, almanacs, and encyclopedias; newspapers (for Follow-Up)
Vocabulary: population map; product map; precipitation map; distribution

LESSON 20.1 Reading and using a population map

1. Discuss the different types of information that students have found on maps, such as time zones, political boundaries, and elevation. Explain that today students will explore maps that show other types of information.
2. Project Map 16. Ask students to read the title of the map. Ask the class what they think a *population map* shows us, and then help them understand that population maps show where people live in a given area and how many people live there. Point out that Map 16 shows the *distribution* of where people live.
3. Ask the class how the symbols help us see which areas have the greatest populations.

(The larger the circle, the greater the population.) Make sure the students understand that the areas with the greatest populations are not necessarily the largest areas.
4. Ask questions such as, "Which areas have the fewest number of people?" "Which areas have more than 5,000,000 people?" "Which areas have 1,000,000 people?"
5. Have students look through their textbooks to find other population maps. Have them compare the different symbols that are used to show population density.

LESSON 20.2 Reading and using a product map

1. Project Map 17. Ask the class to read the title of the map. Explain that this map, which shows the areas where wheat is produced, is called a *product map*. Point out that this map is similar to Map 16 because it also shows distribution.
2. Ask the class to tell you which regions produce the most wheat and which produce the least.

3. Have students suggest a list of other types of products that can be shown on maps. Then have them go on a map hunt to see if they can find the different product maps. Have them compare the different symbols that are used.

LESSON 20.3 Reading and using a precipitation map

1. Project Map 18. Ask the class to tell you what type of map this is. Point out that *precipitation maps* show how much rain, snow, or hail usually falls in a particular place. Explain that Map 18 shows the amount of precipitation that different areas receive.

2. Point to different areas on the map and ask students to tell you how much precipitation that area usually receives.
3. Display Map 11. Ask students to compare the different regions and the types of climates they have. Point out that most of the regions have similar amounts of precipitation.

UNIT 20 continued

LESSON 20.4   Gathering information from different distribution maps

1. Hand out copies of Maps 17 and 18. Ask students to compare the two maps and see if they can draw any conclusions about the amount of precipitation needed to grow wheat. Ask them to consider other factors that might influence the production of wheat, such as elevation and temperature.

2. Have the class look in encyclopedias, social studies textbooks, and almanacs to see if they can find relationships between wheat growth and temperature, rainfall, and elevation.

FOLLOW-UP

1. Help students make a population density map for parts of California. Copy the information from Figure 23 onto the chalkboard. Tell the class this table shows the different populations of some metropolitan areas in California. Have the students read the information aloud.

   Project Map 19. Point out that this map shows the same four areas as the table. Help students locate the different areas on the map. Then draw a small circle on the bottom of the map under the KEY. Explain that this circle will represent one million people.

   Write the information in the key.

   With the students' help, draw the correct number of circles in each area on Map 19. Then ask the class to think of an appropriate title for the map.

2. Have the class find different product maps and precipitation maps in their textbooks. Ask them to compare the product maps with the precipitation maps to see if there is any relationship between the two.

3. Bring in newspapers that contain weather maps and satellite photos. Ask the class to compare the maps and the photos to see if they show the same information.

TABLE 3   POPULATIONS OF SOME CALIFORNIA AREAS (1987)

Region	Population (in millions)
Los Angeles Area	13
Sacramento Area	1
San Diego Area	2
San Francisco Bay Area	6

Figure 23   Table showing populations of some California areas

EXPLORING THE WORLD AROUND US

(Suggested for Grades 5–6)

Unit 21 Using Contour Lines
Lesson 21   Comparing contour lines and cross sections
Follow-Up

Unit 22 Orienting Ourselves to the World
Lesson 22.1   Recognizing the hemispheres
Lesson 22.2   Recognizing latitudes and longitudes
Lesson 22.3   Locating places using latitude and longitude
Lesson 22.4   Recognizing world time zones
Follow-Up

Unit 23 Determining Global Distances
Lesson 23.1   Using great circle routes to determine distance
Lesson 23.2   Using line segments to visualize distance
Follow-Up

Unit 24 Interpreting Different Types of Maps
Lesson 24.1   Reading different map projections
Lesson 24.2   Choosing the appropriate map
Follow-Up

Unit 25 Orienting Ourselves from Space
Lesson 25   Reading and using photos from space
Follow-Up

UNIT 21 *Using Contour Lines*

Objective: To identify elevation using contour lines.
Materials: transparency of Figure 26 (page 52); copies of Figure 26 (for Follow-Up); social studies textbooks (for Follow-Up)
Vocabulary: contour lines; height or altitude scale

LESSON 21 Comparing contour lines and cross sections

1. Review the concept of cross section diagrams. If necessary, use Lesson 14.2 (page 34) or Lesson 19.1 (page 46) to reinforce the concept. Tell the class that today they are going to learn a new way to show elevation on a map.

2. Draw Figure 24 on the chalkboard. Explain that your Drawing A is a cross section of a mountain and that your Drawing B is an aerial view of the same mountain shown by *contour lines*. Tell the class that contour lines show elevation on a map by connecting all the points that are the same height with one line.

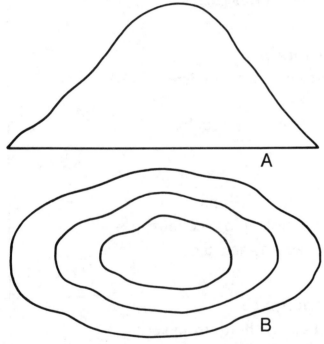

Figure 24 Cross section and contour line diagrams of a mountain

3. Show the class how to "read" the contour lines. Explain that the outside circle on Drawing B represents the base of the mountain. Point out that the width of the outside circle is the same as the width of Drawing A. Then

explain that the center of the inside circle in Drawing B is the same as the peak of the mountain in Drawing A.

4. Now tell the students that sometimes they will see numbers along the contour lines. Explain that these numbers tell the height, or altitude, of each line. Make sure you explain that elevation is measured in feet. Ask the class to pretend that the mountain in your drawing is 3,000 feet high. Then add numbers along the contour lines as shown in Figure 25. Reinforce the idea that all the points along a line are the same height.

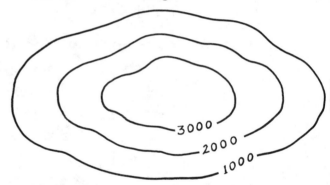

Figure 25 Contour lines showing altitude

5. Project Figure 26. Explain that the drawings in the left-hand column are cross sections of different areas, and the drawings in the right-hand column are contour line drawings of the same areas. As a group, have the class match the lettered cross sections with the numbered contour lines. Explain or have the students explain why the matches they pick seem to be correct. (Answers: 1-C; 2-E; 3-A; 4-F; 5-B; 6-D)

6. Review and clarify all the figures and concepts depicted by the symbols. Also review other ways to show elevation (symbols, color, and shading).

UNIT 21 continued

FOLLOW-UP

1. Distribute copies of Figure 26 to the students. Have the class redo the exercise on their own.
2. Draw several cross section diagrams on the chalkboard. Have students create their own contour line drawings from your diagrams.
3. Have the class go on a map elevation search. Divide the class into groups of four. Give each group a pencil, some paper, and a social studies textbook. Have the groups put the following headings on the paper:

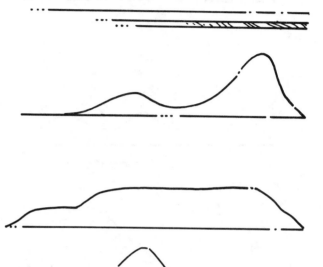

Page #
Map Title
How Elevation Is Shown
Height Scale

Explain each heading, pointing out that some maps give a height or altitude scale as well as a distance scale. Have the teams find as many different elevation maps as they can in a given amount of time. Then give a signal for the class to stop working and evaluate their findings.

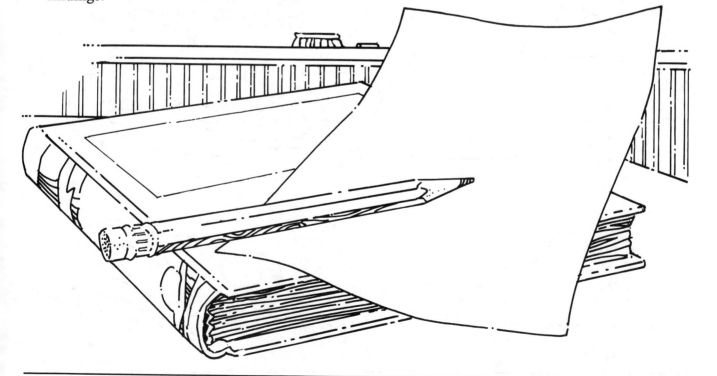

Figure 26 Matching cross sections and contour lines

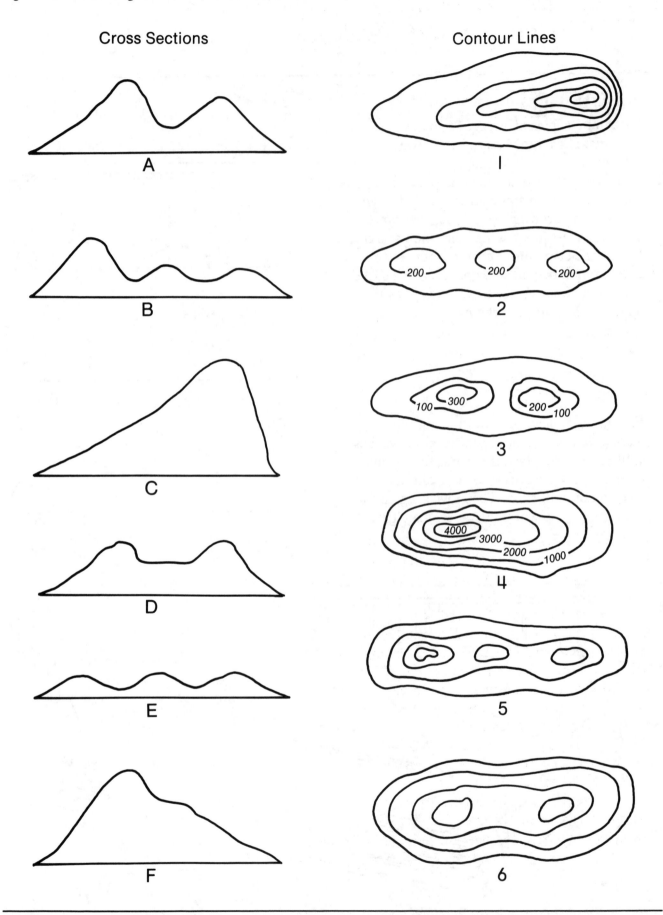

Cross Sections

Contour Lines

Exploring Our World with Maps © 1988

UNIT 22 *Orienting Ourselves to the World*

Objective: To locate places using latitude and longitude.
Materials: transparencies of Maps 20–23 (pages 127–130); copies of Maps 22 and 23, Figure 27 (page 56) and Group Activity C (page 57); globe; string; social studies textbooks (for Follow-Up)
Vocabulary: equator; hemisphere; latitude; longitude; parallels; meridians; prime meridian; index; standard time zones; International Date Line

LESSON 22.1   Recognizing the hemispheres

1. Show the class a globe. Point out the North Pole and the South Pole. Remind the students that halfway between the two poles is an imaginary line around the earth called the *equator*. Take a piece of string and wrap it around the equator. Point out that the string divides the globe into two halves. Explain that we call the half that includes the North Pole the *Northern Hemisphere*, and we call the half that includes the South Pole the *Southern Hemisphere*.

2. Project Map 20. Explain that these maps are flat representations of the globe. If necessary, use the globe to show students how Map 20A shows one half of the globe, while Map 20B shows the other half. Explain that the world can also be divided into Western and Eastern Hemispheres. Tell the class that this is done by grouping continents. Point to Map 20A, and explain that the Western Hemisphere is made up of North America, South America, and half of Antarctica. Then point to Map 20B and show the class that the Eastern Hemisphere is made up of Europe, Asia, Australia, Africa, and half of Antarctica.

3. Ask the class questions about the locations of the different continents. For example, you might ask, "In which two hemispheres do we live?" "In which three hemispheres is Africa?" "In which three hemispheres is Antarctica?" "Which two hemispheres have the most land?"

UNIT 22 continued

LESSON 22.2 Recognizing latitudes and longitudes

1. Project Map 21A. Explain that the lines running east-west are called *parallels* or lines of *latitude*. Point out that these lines mark distances north and south of the equator in degrees. The equator is at 0°, the North Pole is at 90° N, and the South Pole is at 90° S.

2. Show the class the lines of latitude on a globe, so they can see that the lines circle the earth and are parallel to each other.

3. Project Map 21B. Explain that the lines running north-south between the two poles are called *meridians* or lines of *longitude*. Tell the class that there is a special meridian called the *prime meridian*. Lines of longitude mark the distances east and west of the prime meridian in degrees. The prime meridian is at 0°.

4. Show the class the lines of longitude on a globe.

LESSON 22.3 Locating places using latitude and longitude

1. Project Map 22. Point out that this map shows latitude and longitude lines. Remind students that latitude lines run east-west and longitude lines run north-south. Also point out that on this map everything west of the prime meridian from 0° to 180° is thought of as west, and everything east of the prime meridian from 0° to 180° is thought of as east. (If students have problems understanding this concept, use a globe to show them how this division works.)

2. Point out that together, the latitude and longitude lines form a grid. Ask the class if they can explain why this grid would make it easy to find any place on the map. If students do not discover the answer, show them how to find different locations using the lines of latitude and longitude. You might explain, for example, that Ottawa is located at 45° N, 75° W. Run your finger along the latitude line at 45 degrees north of the equator and down the latitude line at 75 degrees west of the prime meridian.

3. Hand out copies of Figure 27 and Map 22. Explain that Figure 27 shows an *index* for Map 22—it tells the latitude and longitude for each city on the map. Pick one of the cities from the index and show the class the city's location on the map. (Note: All locations have been rounded to the nearest degree.)

4. Name a city from the index and have the class find and circle it on their maps. Then ask a student to circle the same city on the transparency. Continue until the class is comfortable locating places using latitude and longitude.

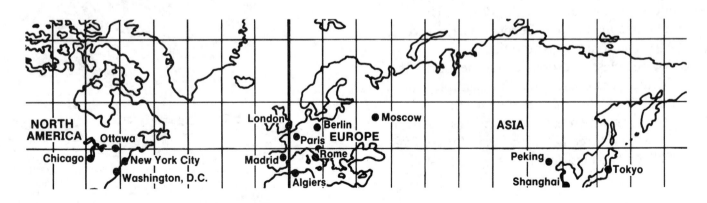

UNIT 22 continued

LESSON 22.4   Recognizing world time zones

1. If necessary, use Lesson 18.1 or Lesson 18.2 (page 43) to review the concept of time zones.

2. Project Map 23. Explain that since the earth makes one complete rotation every 24 hours, there are sunrises and sunsets at different times in different places. Tell the class that most of the world's countries decided to set *standard time zones*. Point out that there are 24 time zones in the world and each zone covers about 15° longitude. Remind students that if you multiply 24 by 15 degrees, you get 360 degrees, which is the complete distance around the world. Also point out that each zone is an hour earlier as you move west.

3. Point out the *International Date Line* on the map. Help students realize that this line is halfway around the world from the prime meridian. Explain that the International Date Line marks the beginning of each new day. When you cross this line going west, you lose a day. When you cross it going east, you gain a day. For example, if it is Monday on the east side, it is Sunday on the west side.

4. Help the students understand the relationship between distance and time by asking questions such as, "If it is noon along the prime meridian, what time is it along the International Date Line?" "If it is noon in London, what time is it in Buenos Aires?" "If it is 7 A.M. in New York City, what time is it in Tokyo?" "If it is 11 A.M. at 15° E longitude, what time is it at 150° W longitude?"

FOLLOW-UP

1. Select a fairly simple map that shows cities and has longitude and latitude lines. Give a map to each group of four students. Have each group prepare a map index of the map. Also have each group write three "quiz" questions about locations on the map. When the groups are finished, compile the questions for the whole class to answer.

2. Distribute copies of Map 23 and Group Activity C to each pair of students. Read the directions to the class. You might want to do the activity aloud with students who have difficulty with it.

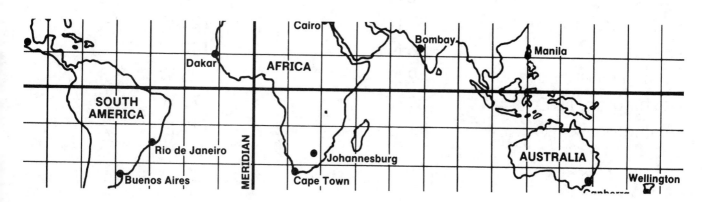

Figure 27   Index for Map 22

City	Latitude (°)	Longitude (°)
Algiers	36 N	3 E
Anchorage	61 N	150 W
Berlin	52 N	13 E
Bombay	19 N	73 E
Buenos Aires	35 S	58 W
Cairo	29 N	31 E
Canberra	35 S	146 E
Cape Town	34 S	18 E
Chicago	42 N	87 W
Dakar	15 N	17 W
Johannesburg	26 S	28 E
Juneau	58 N	134 W
London	51 N	0
Los Angeles	34 N	118 W
Madrid	40 N	3 W
Manila	14 N	120 E
Mexico City	19 N	99 W
Moscow	55 N	37 E
New York	40 N	74 W
Ottawa	45 N	75 W
Paris	49 N	2 E
Peking	40 N	116 E
Rio de Janeiro	22 S	43 W
Rome	42 N	12 E
Shanghai	31 N	121 E
Tokyo	36 N	140 E
Vancouver	49 N	123 W
Washington, D. C.	39 N	77 W
Wellington	41 S	174 E

Group Activity C — Time Zones Around the World

Use Map 23. Circle the letter of the word or numeral that best answers each question.

1. At what longitude is the International Date Line?
   a. 0°
   b. 90° W
   c. 180°
   d. 90° E

2. At what longitude is the prime meridian?
   a. 0°
   b. 90° W
   c. 180°
   d. 90° E

3. If it is Friday in Shanghai, what day is it in New York City?
   a. Thursday
   b. Friday
   c. Saturday
   d. Sunday

4. If it is Saturday afternoon in Rio de Janeiro, what day is it in Rome?
   a. Thursday
   b. Friday
   c. Saturday
   d. Sunday

5. If it is Monday noon in Cairo, what day is it in Los Angeles?
   a. Thursday
   b. Friday
   c. Saturday
   d. Monday

6. If it is Thursday morning in Ottawa, what day is it in Buenos Aires?
   a. Thursday
   b. Friday
   c. Saturday
   d. Sunday

7. If it is 4:00 A.M. in Los Angeles, what time is it in London?
   a. 10:00 A.M.
   b. 11:00 A.M.
   c. 12:00 P.M.
   d. 1:00 P.M.

8. If it is 8:00 P.M. in Peking, what time is it in Shanghai?
   a. 7:00 P.M.
   b. 8:00 P.M.
   c. 9:00 P.M.
   d. 8:00 A.M.

9. If it is 8:00 P.M. in Manila, what time is it in Buenos Aires?
   a. 7:00 P.M.
   b. 8:00 P.M.
   c. 9:00 P.M.
   d. 8:00 A.M.

10. If it is 2:00 P.M. in Johannesberg, what time is it in Cairo?
    a. 1:00 P.M.
    b. 2:00 P.M.
    c. 3:00 P.M.
    d. 2:00 A.M.

Group Activity C continued

11. What is the time difference between Paris and Ottawa?
    a. 5 hours
    c. 7 hours
    b. 6 hours
    d. 8 hours

12. What is the time difference between Tokyo and Rio de Janeiro?
    a. 0 hours
    c. 9 hours
    b. 6 hours
    d. 12 hours

13. What is the time difference between Anchorage and Shanghai?
    a. 0 hours
    c. 9 hours
    b. 6 hours
    d. 12 hours

14. What is the time difference between the International Date Line and the prime meridian?
    a. 0 hours
    c. 9 hours
    b. 6 hours
    d. 12 hours

15. What is the time difference between Rome and Berlin?
    a. 0 hours
    c. 9 hours
    b. 6 hours
    d. 12 hours

16. If it is 4:00 A.M. at 150° W longitude, what time is it at 150° E longitude?
    a. 12:00 P.M.
    c. 4:00 P.M.
    b. 12:00 A.M.
    d. 4:00 A.M.

17. If it is 2:00 A.M. at 30° E longitude, what time is it at 105° W longitude?
    a. 2:00 P.M.
    c. 5:00 P.M.
    b. 2.00 A.M.
    d. 5:00 A.M.

18. If it is 6:00 P.M. at 75° W longitude, what time is it at 90° W longitude?
    a. 5:00 P.M.
    c. 7:00 P.M.
    b. 6:00 P.M.
    d. 8:00 P.M.

19. If it is 1:00 A.M. at 0° longitude, what time is it at 180° longitude?
    a. 1:00 A.M.
    c. 2:00 A.M.
    b. 1:00 P.M.
    d. 12:00 P.M.

20. How many degrees does the earth travel in one hour?
    a. 5 degrees
    c. 15 degrees
    b. 10 degrees
    d. 20 degrees

Exploring Our World with Maps © 1988

UNIT 23 *Determining Global Distances*

Objective: To determine and compare distances in terms of air miles and time.

Materials: globe; string; large piece of butcher paper for each group of four students (for Follow-Up); copies of Map 23 (for Follow-Up)

Vocabulary: great circle routes; air miles; line segments

LESSON 23.1 Using great circle routes to determine distance

1. Show the class how to find *great circle routes* on a globe. Take a piece of string and hold one end at one city (such as London). Then circle the globe with the string until you reach another city (such as New York). Hold up the string so the class can see the stretched-out length. Point out that the string shows the distance between the two points on the globe.

2. Compute the actual distance between the two points using the scale on the globe. Point out that if you were taking an airplane from one place to another, finding the great circle route between the two places will tell you how many *air miles* you would travel.

3. Help students find and compare distances such as the following:
   - What is the shortest route from Moscow to Washington, D.C.?
   - Which city is closer to London—Rio de Janeiro or New York?
   - What is the shortest route from Bogota (Colombia) to Caracas (Venezuela)?
   - Which city is closest to Rome—Cairo, Athens, or Moscow?

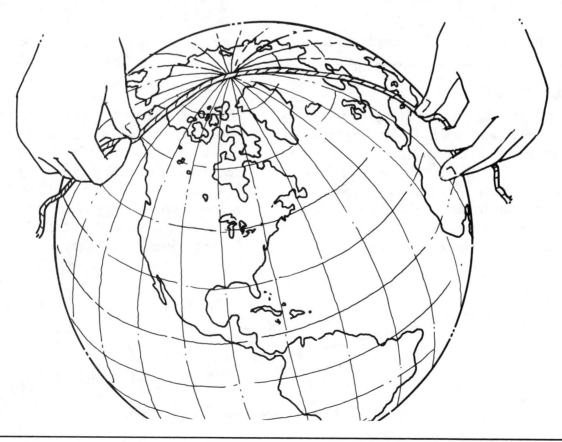

UNIT 23 continued

LESSON 23.2 Using line segments to visualize distance

1. Explain to the class that they are going to learn how to use *line segments* to visualize distance.
2. Draw a dot on the chalkboard. Explain that this dot represents Honolulu. Place another dot some distance away, and explain that the second dot represents San Francisco. Have the class calculate the air miles between Honolulu and San Francisco (approximately 2400 miles). Draw a line between the two dots and write 2400 under the line. (See Figure 28.) Tell the class that this line represents the distance between Honolulu and San Francisco.

3. Now tell the students that you have decided to travel on to Washington, D.C. Ask them where we would plot Washington, D.C. on the chalkboard. Then plot the city and show the distance in air miles. (See Figure 29.) Ask the class which city appears closer to San Francisco.
4. Repeat the exercise using three other cities.

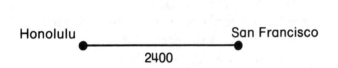

Figure 28 *Air-mile distance between two cities*

Figure 29 *Air-mile distance between three cities*

FOLLOW-UP

1. Tell the class that they are going to become mapmakers for an airline. Divide the class into groups of four. Then have each group use line segments to plot the air miles between three cities (e.g., Tokyo, Paris, and Honolulu). After the students are finished, check their work. Then ask them to add a fourth city to their map (for example, New York). Explain that they will have to pick a "home" city from which to plot the fourth distance. (See Figure 30.) When students are finished, have the class compare the different maps.
2. Hand out copies of Map 23. Have the class repeat Follow-Up 1, plotting the time difference between cities rather than the air miles between cities.

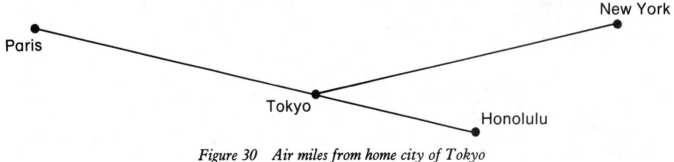

Figure 30 *Air miles from home city of Tokyo*

UNIT 24 *Interpreting Different Types of Maps*

Objective: To determine the uses and limitations of different map projections.

Materials: transparencies of Maps 24 and 25 (pages 131–132); social studies textbooks (for Follow-Up)

Vocabulary: Mercator projection; Lambert's projection; polar projection; interrupted projection

LESSON 24.1   Reading different map projections

1. Remind students that there are many different types of maps. Discuss some maps that have already been introduced—road maps, distribution maps, semantic maps, and relief maps. Help students realize that each map has a specific use.

2. Explain that a flat map cannot show the world as accurately as a globe. To solve this problem, mapmakers draw map *projections,* which show at least one part of the earth accurately. Project Map 24. Tell the class that these maps are different projections of the world and the United States. Each kind of projection serves a different purpose.

3. Discuss the following information with the class:
   - Map 24A is called a *polar projection.* A polar projection shows one of the poles at the center of the map. Ask students which pole is at the center of Map 24A. Point out that north is in the center of the map. Also point out that the latitude lines are shown as circles, while the longitude lines are shown as straight lines that radiate out from the pole.
   - Map 24B is called a "sailor's map" or a *Mercator projection.* On this map all the lines are straight. Have the students point out the latitude and longitude lines.
   - Map 24C is called a *Lambert's projection* or a conic projection. Draw Figure 31 on the chalkboard. Point out that the cone touches the globe on two parallels. A Lambert's projection is a map made of the area between the two parallels. The meridians are drawn

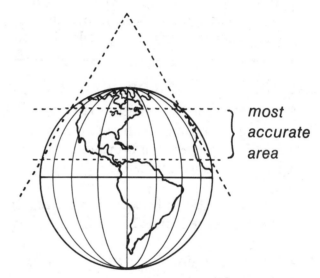

Figure 31   Area mapped in Lambert's Projection

as if they were coming down from the top of the cone. The parallels are drawn as curved lines around the globe.
   - Map 24D is called an *interrupted projection.* Explain that when mapmakers draw the whole earth on a flat surface, the shape of the earth gets distorted. On interrupted projections, space is added between some of the land and water areas so the map will show the areas as accurately as a globe.

4. Help the class discover the uses and limitations of each type of map. Some of these are as follows:
   - Polar projections show true distance between areas, so they are useful to pilots. However, while the size and shape of areas are accurate near the center of the map, they become large and distorted near the edges.

UNIT 24 continued

• Mercator projections are useful to sailors. The sailors can draw a straight line from where they are to where they want to be and then use a compass to set their course. Since a Mercator projection uses straight lines, size and distance are accurate only along the equator. Toward the poles, areas and distances become inaccurate.

• The straight lines on a Lambert's projection are very useful for pilots. They show the shortest flying route between any two places. The area between the two parallels is accurate in distance, direction, size, and shape. Anything outside the parallels becomes distorted.

• An interrupted projection shows the sizes and shapes of specific areas; however, distances and directions are difficult to determine.

5. Sum up the lesson by comparing the size and shape of specific land areas (such as Greenland or Asia). Have the students decide which map projections show the most distortion and the least distortion for each area.

LESSON 24.2   Choosing the appropriate map

1. Project Map 24. Ask the class to decide which map projection would be best to use to find the following types of information:
   • The air distance between two places (A and C)
   • The shortest flight between two places (C)
   • The difference in time between two places (B)
   • The accurate sizes of different areas (D)
   • The direction to sail between places (B)

2. Project Map 25. Repeat step 1, asking questions such as, "Which map would you use to gather information about rainfall in South America?" "Which map would you use to find out about the elevations of an area?" "Which maps are distribution maps?" "Which map shows only one country?"

3. Sum up by discussing the limitations of the different maps.

FOLLOW-UP

1. Play "Map Projection Detective." Project different maps and have students determine the purpose of each map. You might vary the game by asking students to tell you what the major limitations of the different maps are.

2. Have the class find a physical-political map of the world and a population map of the world in their textbooks. Ask the class to tell you the uses and the limitations of both maps. Then tell the class they will be using the maps to answer some questions. Explain that they will have to use both maps to gather the information, since neither map contains enough information on its own. Ask the following types of questions:
   • Do more people live north or south of the equator? Why?
   • Why are some areas in South America more populated than others?
   • Why is there very little population north of 60° N Latitude?
   • Why is Australia more populated along the coasts?

UNIT 25 *Orienting Ourselves from Space*

Objective: To identify the earth and features of the earth in space photos.

Materials: chart of planet positions; transparencies of Photos 3 and 4 (pages 137–138); photos of earth from space (for Follow-Up); science and social studies textbooks (for Follow-Up)

Vocabulary: space photo; satellite photo

LESSON 25   Reading and using photos from space

1. Use a chart of the planets' positions to remind students of the earth's position in the solar system. Point out that astronauts and satellites have taken pictures (*space photos* and *satellite photos*) of the earth from space.
2. Display Photo 3. Explain that this is a picture of the earth that was taken from Apollo 16 in 1972. Ask students to locate North America in the photo. Remind them that the continent will look like it does on a globe. (North America is in the center of the photo, just below the dense cloud layer.)
3. Help students locate other areas, such as the Great Lakes, Florida, Baja California, and part of Central America. Then have the class compare the photo with a map of North America from their textbooks.
4. Project Photo 4. Explain that this picture was taken during an Apollo 7 flight. It shows a hurricane in the Gulf of Mexico. Point out the hurricane pattern and the "eye" of the storm. Ask students how this type of picture can help us predict weather. Discuss the satellite photos we see in weather reports and in newspapers.

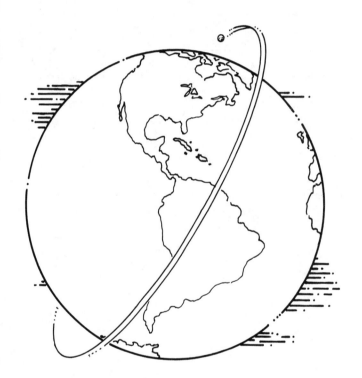

FOLLOW-UP

1. Bring in space photos that show other areas of the world. Ask students to locate specific areas in the photos and on a map.
2. Have students find space and satellite photos in their science and social studies textbooks.

Divide the class into groups of four and let the students search for a given amount of time, such as five minutes. Have each group keep a record of the page number, title, and description of each photo they find.

PART II
Self-Directed Activities

Activity 1 Knowing Directions

Look at the map below. Circle the best answer to each question.

North

lake

West

East

South

1. The car is _____ of the tree.
   a. north   c. east
   b. south   d. west

2. The flower is _____ of the house.
   a. north   c. east
   b. south   d. west

3. The tree is _____ of the car.
   a. north   c. east
   b. south   d. west

4. The house is _____ of the flower.
   a. north   c. east
   b. south   d. west

5. The lake is _____ of the car.
   a. north   c. east
   b. south   d. west

6. The house is _____ of the lake.
   a. north   c. east
   b. south   d. west

7. The lake is _____ of the flower.
   a. north   c. east
   b. south   d. west

8. The tree is _____ of the lake.
   a. north   c. east
   b. south   d. west

Activity 2 **What's the Picture?**

Look at each picture. Circle the word
that best describes each picture.

1. a. sun
   b. fog
   c. cloud

2. a. cloud
   b. tree
   c. shadow

3. a. sun
   b. cloud
   c. tree

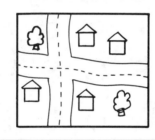
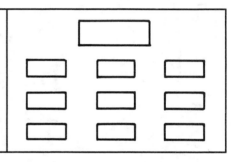

4. a. compass
   b. map
   c. classroom

5. a. compass
   b. map
   c. sun

6. a. shadow
   b. classroom
   c. compass

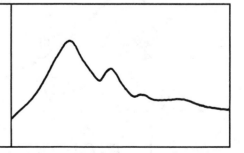

7. a. tree
   b. cloud
   c. compass

8. a. map
   b. classroom
   c. house

9. a. sun
   b. shadow
   c. mountain

Activity 3 Find the Directions!

Read down to find each direction word. Circle it. Then check it off in the box below.

```
B S N Z S T W Y
R Z E O O T B E
A A A N U L L D
N R S K T L R O
O G T S H A L W
R R F G S W E N
T I W U L E F O
H G O P R S T R
Z H G I M T N L
N T A Y O V A S
```

RIGHT	UP	NORTH	EAST
LEFT	DOWN	SOUTH	WEST

Activity 4 Finding Your Way Around School

Use the map to answer the questions.
Circle the best answer to each
question.

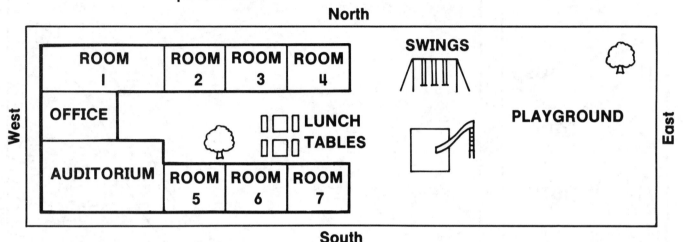

1. How many classrooms are
   there?
   a. 6   c. 10
   b. 7   d. 12

2. Rooms 1, 2, and 3 are on the
   _____ side of the school.
   a. north   c. east
   b. south   d. west

3. The office is on the _____ side
   of the school.
   a. north   c. east
   b. south   d. west

4. Which room is closest to the
   swings?
   a. Room 2   c. Room 4
   b. Room 3   d. Room 5

5. What side of the school is the
   playground on?
   a. north   c. east
   b. south   d. west

6. The shortest way from Room
   2 to Room 5 is to go _____ .
   a. north   c. east
   b. south   d. west

7. The shortest way from Room
   1 to the auditorium is to go

   _____ .
   a. north   c. east
   b. south   d. west

Activity 5 **Using Symbols**

Use the map and key to fill in the blanks below.

1. There are two _____ by the road.

2. The road goes from the house to the

    _____ .

3. There is a _____ next to the park.

4. How many lakes are there on this map?

    _____ .

5. Are there any flowers near the road?

    _____ .

6. Draw a tree next to the house.

7. Color the road yellow.

8. Color the lake blue.

Activity 6 **Knowing How to Orient Yourself**

Circle the answer that best completes each sentence.

1. The opposite of north is
   _____ .
   a. north   c. east
   b. south   d. west

2. The opposite of east is _____ .
   a. north   c. east
   b. south   d. west

3. Usually, a compass needle will point _____ .
   a. north   c. east
   b. south   d. west

4. If it is a sunny day, you can tell directions by using _____ .
   a. a compass
   b. your shadow
   c. both of these
   d. none of these

5. If it is a cloudy day, you can tell directions by using _____ .
   a. a compass
   b. your shadow
   c. both of these
   d. none of these

6. The symbol NE means that the direction is between
   _____ .
   a. north and east
   b. north and west
   c. south and east
   d. south and west

7. The symbol SW means that the direction is between
   _____ .
   a. north and east
   b. north and west
   c. south and east
   d. south and west

8. The main directions are called _____ .
   a. imperial directions
   b. intermediate directions
   c. cardinal directions
   d. none of these

9. The in-between directions are known as _____ .
   a. imperial directions
   b. intermediate directions
   c. cardinal directions
   d. none of these

Activity 7   **Using Keys to Unlock Maps**

Use Maps 2 and 3. Circle the best
answer to each question.

1. Which objects appear in
   both map keys?
   a. schools and hospitals
   b. schools and houses
   c. houses and stores
   d. stores and hospitals

2. Which map has a symbol
   for a hospital in its key?
   a. Map 2   c. both maps
   b. Map 3   d. neither map

3. Which map has a symbol
   for a store in its key?
   a. Map 2   c. both maps
   b. Map 3   d. neither map

4. Which map has a symbol
   for a gas station in its key?
   a. Map 2   c. both maps
   b. Map 3   d. neither map

5. Which map has a symbol
   for a library in its key?
   a. Map 2   c. both maps
   b. Map 3   d. neither map

6. Which map has a symbol
   for a house in its key?
   a. Map 2   c. both maps
   b. Map 3   d. neither map

7. Which map shows water?
   a. Map 2   c. both maps
   b. Map 3   d. neither map

8. Which map shows a fire
   station?
   a. Map 2   c. both maps
   b. Map 3   d. neither map

9. Which map uses this exact
   symbol:
   a. Map 2   c. both maps
   b. Map 3   d. neither map

10. Which map uses this exact
    symbol:
    a. Map 2   c. both maps
    b. Map 3   d. neither map

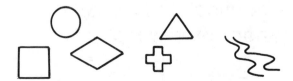

Exploring Our World with Maps © 1988

Activity 8   **Finding Places at the Zoo**

Use Map 26. Circle the answer that best completes each sentence.

1. The entrance to the zoo is on the ____ side.
   a. north   c. east
   b. south   d. west

2. As you enter the zoo, the ____ are directly in front of you.
   a. birds   c. lions
   b. tigers   d. chimpanzees

3. If you turn east after entering the zoo, the ____ will be on your right.
   a. hippos   c. birds
   b. seals   d. gift shop

4. You decide you want to see the zebras, which are in the ____ corner of the zoo.
   a. northwest   c. southwest
   b. northeast   d. southeast

5. If you look directly north from the zebras' cage, you will see the ____ .
   a. seals   c. hippos
   b. tigers   d. giraffes

6. You stop to look at the giraffes, and then go ____ to see the leopards.
   a. north   c. east
   b. south   d. west

7. You move west one cage and find you are looking at the ____ .
   a. hippos
   b. tigers
   c. lions
   d. popcorn stand

8. While you are staring at the cage, you hear a horrible crashing noise behind you. You turn around and see the ____ .
   a. gorillas
   b. tigers
   c. lions
   d. popcorn stand

Name _____

Activity 8 continued

9. You look at the lions, and then move ____ one cage to see the snakes.
   - a. north
   - b. south
   - c. east
   - d. west

10. To see the seals you need to walk ____ from the snakes' pit.
    - a. north
    - b. south
    - c. east
    - d. west

11. If you go east from the seals, you will see the ____ .
    - a. birds
    - b. snakes
    - c. chimpanzees
    - d. elephants

12. You realize that it is getting late and you have not seen all the animals. You really want to see the elephants which are in the ____ corner of the zoo.
    - a. northwest
    - b. northeast
    - c. southwest
    - d. southeast

13. On your way to the exit, you decide to stop at the ____ which is in between the elephants and the entrance.
    - a. hippos
    - b. birds
    - c. zebras
    - d. gift shop

14. It is time for you to leave, so you walk out the exit on the ____ side of the zoo.
    - a. north
    - b. south
    - c. east
    - d. west

Exploring Our World with Maps © 1988

Activity 9   **Making Your Own Semantic Map**

Use Map 3. Write the name of each building on the map in the correct box on the semantic map below.

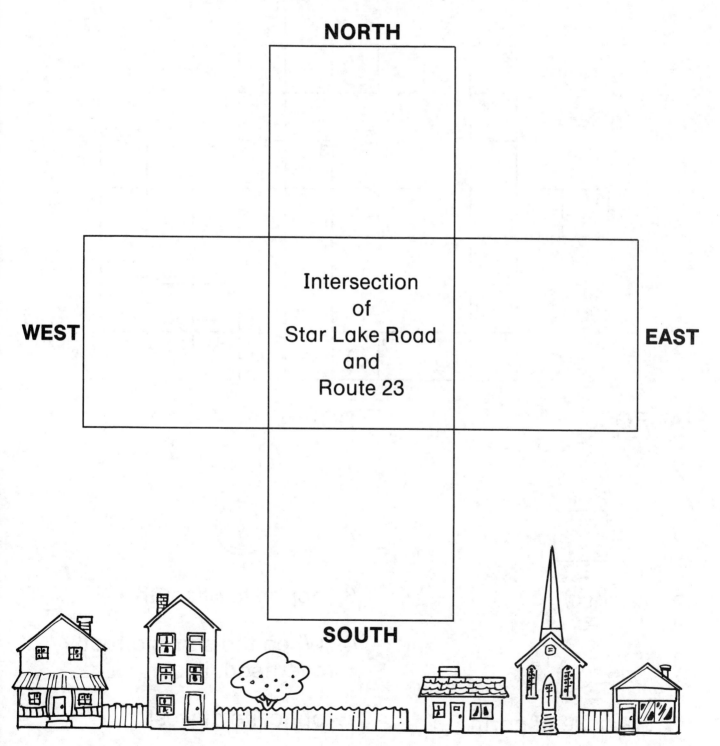

NORTH

WEST   **EAST**

Intersection
of
Star Lake Road
and
Route 23

SOUTH

Activity 10 **A Picture Clue Crossword Puzzle**

Use the clues to solve the puzzle.
Write one letter in each box.

ACROSS

2.

5.

6.

8.

9. opposite of north

DOWN

1.

2.

3. opposite of south

4. When the sun is directly overhead, it is _____ .

7. opposite of west

Exploring Our World with Maps © 1988

Activity 11 **Finding Places on a Road Map**

Use the map below to answer the questions.
Circle the best answer to each question.

KEY

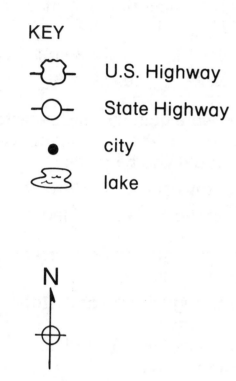

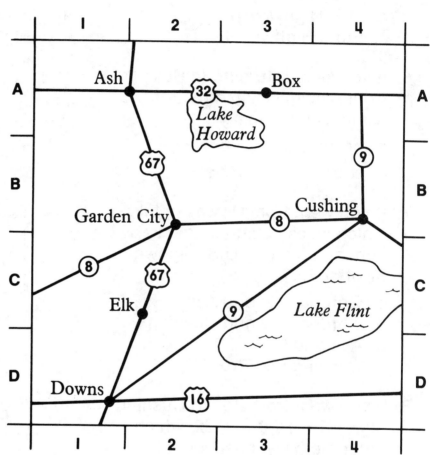

1. What city is located in square A-3?

   a. Box   c. Garden City
   b. Cushing   d. Elk

2. What city is located in square B-2?

   a. Box   c. Garden City
   b. Cushing   d. Elk

3. What city is located in square B-4?

   a. Box   c. Garden City
   b. Cushing   d. Elk

4. What grid square is Downs located in?

   a. C-1   c. D-1
   b. C-2   d. D-2

Activity 11 continued

5. If you were going from Ash to Box, which highway would you take?

   a. U.S. Highway 67
   b. U.S. Highway 32
   c. U.S. Highway 16
   d. State Highway 8

6. If you were returning to Box from Ash, in which direction would you be going?

   a. north   c. east
   b. south   d. west

7. If you went from Downs to Elk, which cities could you get to by continuing along U.S. Highway 67 after Elk?

   a. Garden City and Ash
   b. Garden City and Cushing
   c. Ash and Box
   d. Cushing and Box

8. If you went from Box to Cushing along U.S. Highway 32, which other highway must you take?

   a. U.S. Highway 67
   b. U.S. Highway 16
   c. State Highway 9
   d. State Highway 8

9. Which city is closest to Lake Howard?

   a. Ash   c. Cushing
   b. Box   d. Downs

10. Which city is farthest from Lake Flint?

    a. Ash   c. Cushing
    b. Box   d. Downs

11. If you were going from Downs to Cushing, in what general direction would you be going?

    a. southwest   c. northwest
    b. southeast   d. northeast

12. Which two highways intersect in Garden City?

    a. U.S. Highway 67 and State Highway 9
    b. U.S. Highway 67 and U.S. Highway 32
    c. State Highway 8 and U.S. Highway 67
    d. State Highway 8 and State Highway 9

Activity 12 Finding Distances on a Road Map

Use the map below to answer the questions.
Circle the best answer to each question.

KEY

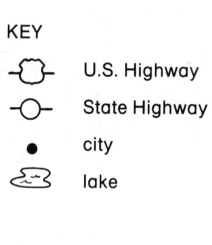

- U.S. Highway
- State Highway
- city
- lake

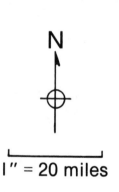

N

1" = 20 miles

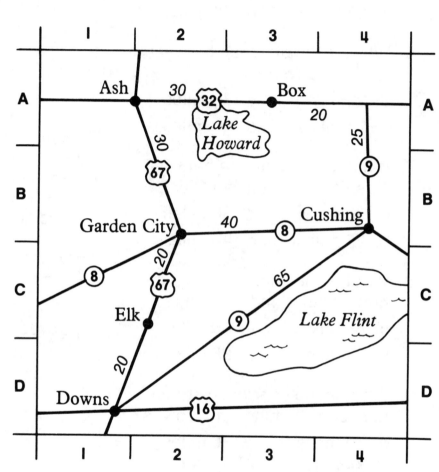

1. On this map, how many miles does one inch show?

   a. 10   c. 30
   b. 20   d. 40

2. Which highway connects Downs and Cushing?

   a. U.S. Highway 16
   b. U.S. Highway 67
   c. State Highway 8
   d. State Highway 9

3. Which highway connects Elk and Ash?

   a. U.S. Highway 16
   b. U.S. Highway 67
   c. State Highway 8
   d. State Highway 9

4. What is the distance between Ash and Garden City?

   a. 20 miles   c. 30 miles
   b. 25 miles   d. 40 miles

5. What is the distance between Garden City and Elk?

   a. 20 miles   c. 30 miles

   b. 25 miles   d. 40 miles

6. What is the distance between Elk and Downs?

   a. 20 miles   c. 30 miles

   b. 25 miles   d. 40 miles

7. What is the distance between Cushing and Garden City?

   a. 20 miles   c. 30 miles

   b. 25 miles   d. 40 miles

8. What is the shortest distance between Elk and Cushing?

   a. 60 miles   c. 80 miles

   b. 65 miles   d. 85 miles

9. What is the shortest distance between Cushing and Downs?

   a. 60 miles   c. 80 miles

   b. 65 miles   d. 85 miles

10. If you went from Cushing to Ash, by way of Box, how far would you travel?

   a. 60 miles   c. 70 miles

   b. 65 miles   d. 75 miles

11. If you returned to Cushing from Ash, by way of Garden City, how far would you travel?

   a. 60 miles   c. 70 miles

   b. 65 miles   d. 75 miles

12. Complete the mileage chart below. Remember to use the shortest distances between the different places.

	Ash	Box	Cushing	Downs	Elk	Garden City
Ash						
Box						
Cushing						
Downs						
Elk						
Garden City						

Activity 13 Comparing Shapes and Sizes

Use the maps below to answer the questions.
Circle the best answer to each question.
Use these state maps to answer questions 1–6.

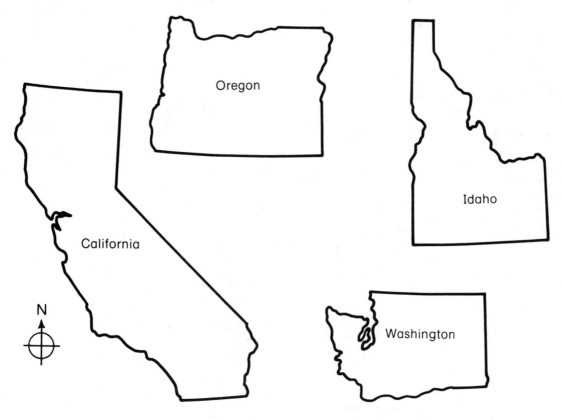

1. Which state has the longest north-south distance?
   a. California   c. Oregon
   b. Idaho   d. Washington

2. Which state has the shortest north-south distance?
   a. California   c. Oregon
   b. Idaho   d. Washington

3. Which state has the longest east-west distance overall?
   a. California   c. Oregon
   b. Idaho   d. Washington

4. Which state has the shortest east-west distance overall?
   a. California   c. Oregon
   b. Idaho   d. Washington

5. Which state is the largest in size?
   a. California   c. Oregon
   b. Idaho   d. Washington

6. Which state is the smallest in size?
   a. California   c. Oregon
   b. Idaho   d. Washington

Name _____

Activity 13 continued

Use these maps to answer questions 7–12.

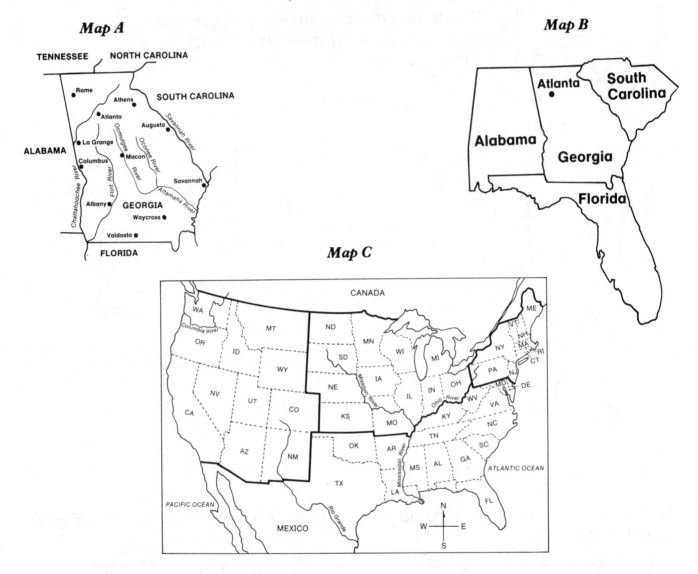

Map A

Map B

Map C

7. Which map shows the most area?
   a. Map A   b. Map B   c. Map C

8. Which map shows the least area?
   a. Map A   b. Map B   c. Map C

9. Which map shows the most detail of Georgia?
   a. Map A   b. Map B   c. Map C

10. Which map shows the least detail of Georgia?
    a. Map A   b. Map B   c. Map C

11. Which map does not show four southern states?
    a. Map A   b. Map B   c. Map C

12. Which map would be best to use to locate cities in Georgia?
    a. Map A   b. Map B   c. Map C

Exploring Our World with Maps © 1988

Name _____

Activity 14 Exploring Landforms in South America

Use Map 27. Circle the best answer to each question.

1. What does this map show?
   a. countries
   b. landforms
   c. South America
   d. all of these

2. Where are most of the mountains located?
   a. west coast
   b. east coast
   c. south coast
   d. inland

3. Where are most of the plains located?
   a. west coast
   b. east coast
   c. south coast
   d. inland

4. Where is the largest plateau located?
   a. west coast
   b. east coast
   c. south coast
   d. inland

5. Which country seems to have the lowest elevation?
   a. Ecuador
   b. Chile
   c. Argentina
   d. Uruguay

6. Which country seems to have the highest elevation?
   a. Ecuador
   b. Chile
   c. Argentina
   d. Uruguay

7. Chile is mostly _____ .
   a. mountains
   b. plateaus
   c. hills
   d. plains or lowlands

8. French Guiana is mostly _____ .
   a. mountains
   b. plateaus
   c. hills
   d. plains or lowlands

9. Paraguay is mostly _____ .
   a. mountains
   b. plateaus
   c. hills
   d. plains or lowlands

10. What symbol is used to indicate hills?
    a. dots
    b. lines
    c. shading
    d. none of these

11. What symbol is used to show mountains?
    a. dots
    b. lines
    c. shading
    d. none of these

12. What symbol is used to indicate plains?
    a. dots
    b. lines
    c. shading
    d. none of these

Activity 15 Using Map Terms: A Crossword Puzzle

Use the clues to solve the puzzle below. Write one letter in each box.

Activity 15 continued

ACROSS

1. Shows distance in a map key
5. A grown male
8. North or South _____
9. Picture
11. Land away from a coast
13. Opposite of *out of*
14. Require
15. Everything
17. Units of distance
20. Hills and plains are two _____ of landforms.
22. Short for sister
23. The foot of a cat
25. It's = _____ is
26. A drawing of a place
28. Monkey
29. Height (abbreviation)
30. She _____ a knot.
31. Height

DOWN

1. To rotate
2. An ice-cream _____
3. A narrow street
4. Show the way or a mineral
5. Monday (abbreviation)
6. American Telephone and Telegraph (abbreviation)
7. Midday
10. One type of landform
12. Moist
16. Falsehoods
18. Oregon has an almost square _____ .
19. A hole in the ground
21. The yes used in voting
22. Area
23. What you feel when you hurt yourself
24. Opposite of *east*
26. Music Television (abbreviation)
27. A cat makes a good _____ .
29. Opposite of *she*
30. You can use grids _____ locate places on a map.

Name _____

Activity 16 **A Map Word Search**

The map words in the list are all hidden some-
where in the puzzle. Some words go from left to
right, some go from bottom to top, and some go
diagonally. Each time you find a word, circle it
in the puzzle and make a check next to it on the
list. The word AREA has been done for you.

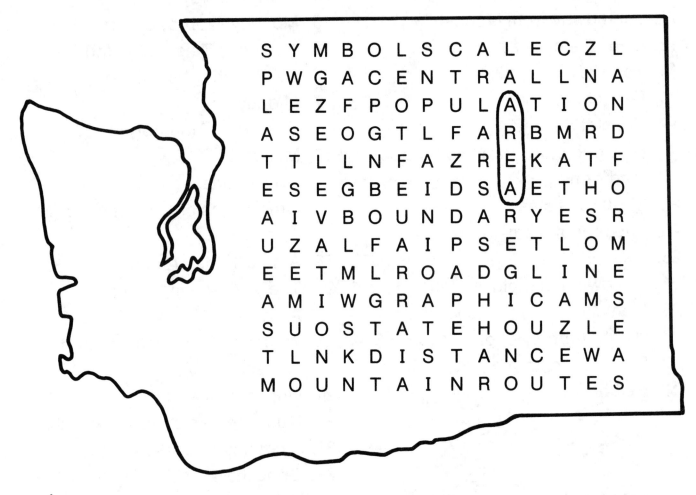

```
S  Y  M  B  O  L  S  C  A  L  E  C  Z  L
P  W  G  A  C  E  N  T  R  A  L  L  N  A
L  E  Z  F  P  O  P  U  L  A  T  I  O  N
A  S  E  O  G  T  L  F  A  R  B  M  R  D
T  T  L  L  N  F  A  Z  R  E  K  A  T  F
E  S  E  G  B  E  I  D  S  A  E  T  H  O
A  I  V  B  O  U  N  D  A  R  Y  E  S  R
U  Z  A  L  F  A  I  P  S  E  T  L  O  M
E  E  T  M  L  R  O  A  D  G  L  I  N  E
A  M  I  W  G  R  A  P  H  I  C  A  M  S
S  U  O  S  T  A  T  E  H  O  U  Z  L  E
T  L  N  K  D  I  S  T  A  N  C  E  W  A
M  O  U  N  T  A  I  N  R  O  U  T  E  S
```

✓ AREA	GRAPHIC	MOUNTAIN	SCALE
BOUNDARY	GRIDS	NORTH	SIZE
CENTRAL	HILLS	PLAIN	SLOPES
CLIMATE	KEY	PLATEAU	STATE
DISTANCE	LANDFORM	POPULATION	SYMBOL
EAST	LINE	REGION	TIME
ELEVATION	LOWLAND	ROAD	WEST
FAR	MAP	ROUTES	ZONE

Exploring Our World with Maps © 1988

Activity 17 **Working with Scale and Distance**

Use Map 12, a piece of paper, and a pencil to answer the questions. Circle the best answer each question.

1. Which type of scale is shown on this map?
   a. graphic scale
   b. statement of scale
   c. ratio scale
   d. none of these

2. Which units of distance appear in the scale?
   a. feet and miles
   b. miles
   c. kilometers
   d. miles and kilometers

3. Which type of map is Map 12?
   a. physical   c. road
   b. semantic   d. air-route

4. If you drove from Des Moines to Cedar Falls, going through Iowa Falls, approximately how far would you travel?
   a. 90 miles   c. 130 miles
   b. 110 miles   d. 160 miles

5. If you drove back from Cedar Falls to Des Moines, going through Marshalltown, approximately how far would you travel?
   a. 100 miles   c. 130 miles
   b. 115 miles   d. 145 miles

6. If you drove from Ottumwa to Mt. Pleasant, how far would you travel?
   a. 30 miles   c. 70 miles
   b. 50 miles   d. 90 miles

7. How many kilometers would this trip be?
   a. 75   c. 85
   b. 80   d. 90

8. If you continued driving from Mt. Pleasant to Iowa City, about how far would you travel?
   a. 32 miles   c. 55 miles
   b. 43 miles   d. 75 miles

9. About how many kilometers would this trip be?
   a. 45   c. 75
   b. 60   d. 90

10. If you could fly directly from Ottumwa to Iowa City, how many miles would you fly?
    a. 40   c. 65
    b. 50   d. 85

11. If you could fly directly from Iowa City to Dubuque, how many miles would you fly?
    a. 40   c. 60
    b. 45   d. 75

Activity 18 Finding States on a United States Map: A Word Puzzle

A. Use Map 10. Fill in the blanks with letters to spell the names of American states. One letter is given for each state to help you.

1.   _ _ _ S _ _

2.   _ _ _ _ _ _ T _ _ _ _

3.   _ _ A _ _ _ _

4.   _ _ N _ _ _ _

5.   _ _ _ D _

6.   _ _ A _ _

7.   _ R _ _ _ _

8.   D _ _ _ _ _ _ _

9.   _ _ _ _ _ _ _ _ _ _ T _

10.   _ _ _ I _ _ _

11.   _ _ _ M _ _ _ _

12.   _ _ _ _ E _ _ _ _ _

13.   _ _ _ Z _ _ _

14.   O _ _ _ _ _ _ _

15.   _ _ _ _ _ N _

16.   _ E _ _ _

17.   _ _ S _ _ _ _ _

Activity 18 continued

B. Use Map 14. Find out in which time zone or time zones each state you named in part A is located. Write the names of the time zone or time zones next to the number that matches the number of the state.

1. _____

2. _____

3. _____

4. _____

5. _____

6. _____

7. _____

8. _____

9. _____

10. _____

11. _____

12. _____

13. _____

14. _____

15. _____

16. _____

17. _____

Activity 19 Matching Cross Sections and Word Descriptions

Match each section of the cross section diagram below with the most appropriate word description. Write the letter of the section in the blank next to the description. You may use a letter more than once.

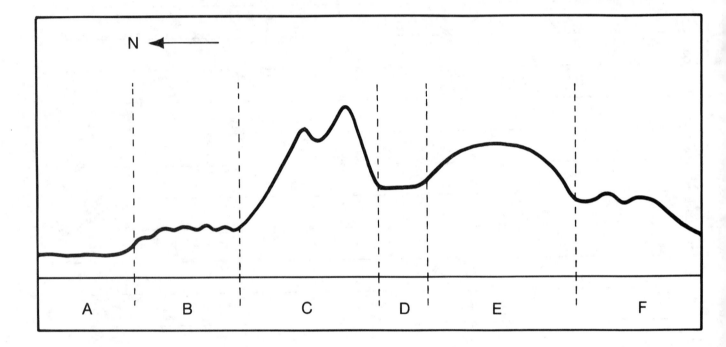

1. Plateau _____

2. Plains or lowlands _____

3. Mountain with the steepest southern slope _____

4. Mountain with the steepest northern slope _____

5. Rolling hills _____

6. Hill with two gentle peaks _____

7. Mountain with two peaks _____

8. Southernmost mountain _____

9. Northernmost foothills _____

10. Mountain with gentle slope _____

Activity 20   Using Maps to Gather Information

Use Maps 15–18 to answer the questions. Circle
the best answer to each question.

1. Which map would you use to
   find out about wheat production?
   a. Map 15   c. Map 17
   b. Map 16   d. Map 18

2. Which map would you use to
   find out about precipitation?
   a. Map 15   c. Map 17
   b. Map 16   d. Map 18

3. Which map would you use to
   find out about landforms?
   a. Map 15   c. Map 17
   b. Map 16   d. Map 18

4. Which map would you use to
   find out about population?
   a. Map 15   c. Map 17
   b. Map 16   d. Map 18

5. Which region of the United States
   produces the most wheat?
   a. The West   c. The Midwest
   b. The South   d. The Northeast

6. Which region of the United States
   gets mostly 10–20 inches of rain?
   a. The West   c. The Midwest
   b. The South   d. The Northeast

7. Which state is in an area that gets
   over 50 inches of rain a year?
   a. Montana   c. Arizona
   b. Minnesota   d. Mississippi

8. Which state is in an area that gets
   mostly 21 to 30 inches of rain a
   year?
   a. Montana   c. Arizona
   b. Minnesota   d. Mississippi

Activity 20 continued

9. Which state is in an area that gets mostly 10 to 20 inches of rain a year?

   a. Montana   c. Arizona

   b. Minnesota   d. Mississippi

10. How many people live in the Dallas area?

    a. 1,000,000   c. 4,500,000

    b. 3,000,000   d. 7,500,000

11. How many people live in the Los Angeles area?

    a. 1,000,000   c. 4,500,000

    b. 3,000,000   d. 7,500,000

12. How many people live in the Columbus area?

    a. 1,000,000   c. 4,500,000

    b. 3,000,000   d. 7,500,000

13. How many areas have a population of 2,000,000?

    a. 1   c. 3

    b. 2   d. 4

14. How many areas have a population of 10,000,000?

    a. 1   c. 3

    b. 2   d. 4

Activity 21 **Getting to the Top with Cross Sections and Contours**

A. Write the letter of each cross section or contour line drawing in the space next to its appropriate word description.

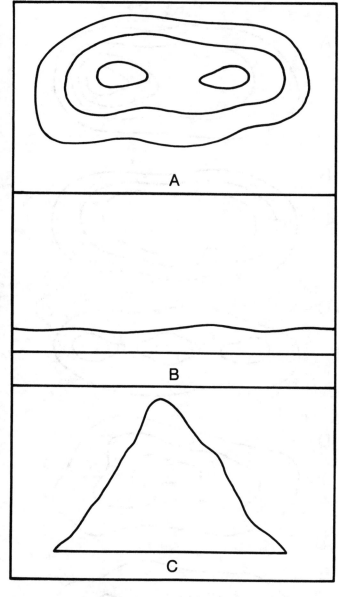

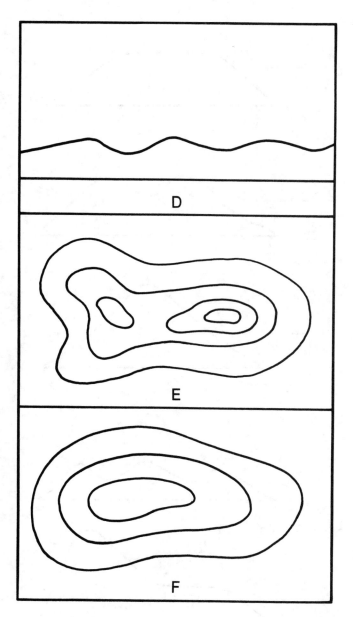

_____ 1. rolling hills

_____ 2. high mountain with steep slopes

_____ 3. lowlands or plains

_____ 4. two peaks with one peak higher

_____ 5. round hill with two peaks

_____ 6. mountain with gentle slopes

Activity 21 continued

B. Write the letter of each contour in the space next to the cross section that most closely matches it.

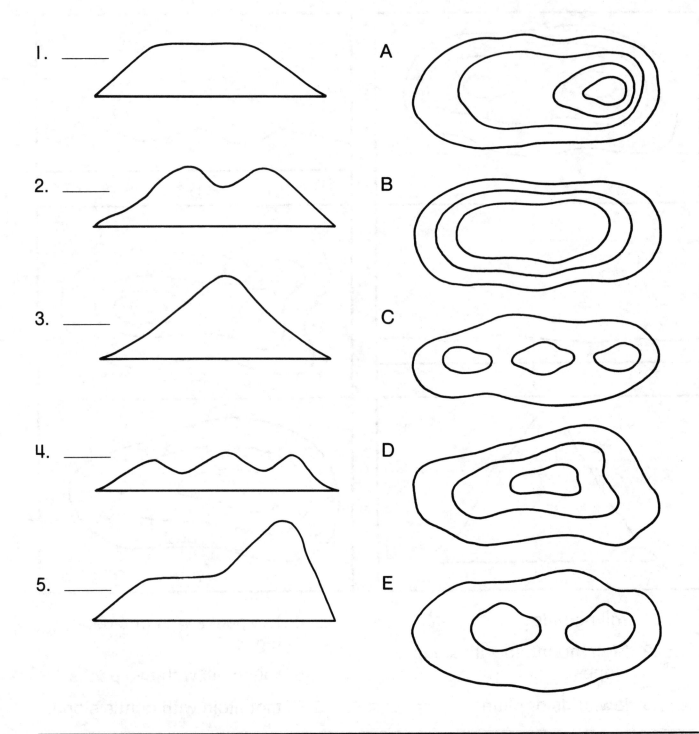

1. _____

2. _____

3. _____

4. _____

5. _____

A

B

C

D

E

Activity 22   Finding Places Using Longitude and Latitude

Use Map 22. Circle the best answer to each question.

1. What is the latitude reading at the equator?
   a. 0°
   b. 5°
   c. 10°
   d. 15°

2. What is the latitude reading at Dakar?
   a. 5° N
   b. 15° N
   c. 5° S
   d. 15° S

3. What is the latitude reading at Peking?
   a. 30° S
   b. 40° S
   c. 30° S
   d. 40° N

4. What is the latitude reading at Los Angeles?
   a. 34° N
   b. 41° N
   c. 34° S
   d. 41° S

5. What is the latitude reading at Cape Town?
   a. 34° N
   b. 41° N
   c. 34° S
   d. 41° S

6. What distances do longitudes mark?
   a. degrees north and south
   b. degrees east and west
   c. both a and b
   d. none of the above

7. What is the longitude reading at London?
   a. 0°
   b. 5°
   c. 10°
   d. 15°

8. What is the longitude reading at Algiers?
   a. 3° E
   b. 10° E
   c. 3° W
   d. 10° W

9. What is the longitude reading at Madrid?
   a. 3° E
   b. 10° E
   c. 3° W
   d. 10° W

10. What is the longitude reading at Tokyo?
    a. 130° E
    b. 140° E
    c. 150° E
    d. 130° W

11. What is the location of Bombay?
    a. 19° N Latitude
       73° E Longitude
    b. 40° N Latitude
       3° W Longitude
    c. 19° N Latitude
       99° W Longitude
    d. 22° S Latitude
       43° W Longitude

Activity 22 continued

12. What is the location of Rio de Janeiro?

    a. 19° N Latitude
       73° E Longitude

    b. 40° N Latitude
       3° W Longitude

    c. 19° N Latitude
       99° W Longitude

    d. 22° S Latitude
       43° W Longitude

13. Where is Cairo located?

    a. 29° N Latitude
       31° E Longitude

    b. 40° N Latitude
       13° E Longitude

    c. 40° N Latitude
       74° W Longitude

    d. 45° N Latitude
       75° W Longitude

14. Where is Ottawa located?

    a. 29° N Latitude
       31° E Longitude

    b. 40° N Latitude
       13° E Longitude

    c. 40° N Latitude
       74° W Longitude

    d. 45° N Latitude
       77° W Longitude

15. Where is New York City located?

    a. 29° N Latitude
       31° E Longitude

    b. 40° N Latitude
       13° E Longitude

    c. 40° N Latitude
       74° W Longitude

    d. 45° N Latitude
       75° W Longitude

16. Which city is located at 31° N Latitude and 121° E Longitude?

    a. Cairo   c. Shanghai

    b. Los Angeles   d. Cape Town

17. Which city is located at 34° S Latitude and 18° E Longitude?

    a. Cairo   c. Shanghai

    b. Los Angeles   d. Cape Town

18. Which city is located at 34° N Latitude and 118° W Longitude?

    a. Cairo   c. Shanghai

    b. Los Angeles   d. Cape Town

19. Which city is located at 58° N Latitude and 134° W Longitude?

    a. Cairo   c. Shanghai

    b. Juneau   d. Buenos Aires

20. Which city is located at 29° N Latitude and 31° E Longitude?

    a. Cairo   c. Shanghai

    b. Juneau   d. Buenos Aires

Activity 23 Drawing Conclusions from Different Sources

Use Map 23 and a globe. Read the story below. Then circle or write the best answer to each question.

Story

Melissa lived in Los Angeles. She had always wanted to go to Cairo. So, she went to a travel agent who said that Melissa would have to fly from Los Angeles to New York and then from New York to Cairo.

Melissa left on a Tuesday. The plane took off at noon, and arrived in New York at 9:00 P.M. When the plane landed, the pilot reminded the passengers to reset their watches.

The flight to Cairo left at midnight. After a 14-hour flight, the plane landed in Cairo.

1. Where does Melissa live?
   a. Cairo   c. New York
   b. Los Angeles d. Africa

2. When Melissa's plane left Los Angeles, what time was it in New York?
   a. 3:00 P.M.   c. 3:00 A.M.
   b. 9:00 P.M.   d. 9:00 A.M.

3. When Melissa's plane left Los Angeles, what time was it in Cairo?
   a. 2:00 P.M.   c. 2:00 A.M.
   b. 10:00 P.M.   d. 10:00 A.M.

4. What is the time difference between Los Angeles and New York?
   a. 1 hour   c. 5 hours
   b. 3 hours   d. 7 hours

5. What is the time difference between New York and Cairo?
   a. 1 hour   c. 5 hours
   b. 3 hours   d. 7 hours

6. On what day did Melissa's plane arrive in Cairo?
   a. Monday   c. Wednesday
   b. Tuesday   d. Thursday

7. At what time did Melissa's plane land in Cairo?
   a. 7:00 A.M.   c. 9:00 A.M.
   b. 7:00 P.M.   d. 9:00 P.M.

8. Use the globe to find the distance between Los Angeles and New York, and New York and Cairo. Make a line segment drawing that shows the air mile distances. Remember to put New York in the middle.

Name _____

Activity 24 **Exploring Different Maps**

Use Map 24 to answer questions 1–8. Use Map 25 to answer questions 9–14. Circle the best answer to each question.

1. What type of projection is Map 24A?

   a. Interrupted   c. polar

   b. Mercator   d. none of these

2. Where is north on Map 24A?

   a. the circles

   b. at the center

   c. away from the center

   d. at the top of the page

3. On Map 24A, what direction is North America from the center point of the map?

   a. north   c. east

   b. south   d. west

4. On Map 24A, what direction is Europe from the center point of the map?

   a. north   c. east

   b. south   d. west

5. Who would find Map 24B useful?

   a. pilots   c. sailors

   b. drivers   d. hikers

6. Who would find Map 24C useful?

   a. pilots   c. sailors

   b. drivers   d. hikers

7. Which projection shows the greatest distortion of Asia?

   a. Map 24A   c. Map 24C

   b. Map 24B   d. Map 24D

8. What is difficult to determine on an interrupted projection?

   a. shape and distance

   b. shape and size

   c. direction and distance

   d. direction and size

Exploring Our World with Maps © 1988

Activity 24 continued

9. What type of map is Map 25A?
   a. distribution map
   b. topological map
   c. rainfall distribution map
   d. all of these

10. Which hemisphere is the continent shown in Map 25A a part of?
    a. Western Hemisphere
    b. Northern Hemisphere
    c. Southern Hemisphere
    d. all of the above

11. Which map is a physical map?
    a. Map 25A
    b. Map 25B
    c. Map 25C
    d. none of these

12. What type of map is 25B?
    a. distribution map
    b. product map
    c. political map
    d. all of these

13. In how many places can lead be found?
    a. 6   c. 10
    b. 7   d. 12

14. How does Map 25C show elevation?
    a. with contour lines
    b. with symbols
    c. with contour lines and numbers
    d. with shading and numbers

Name

Activity 25 Filling in the Blanks: A Crossword Puzzle

Use the clues to solve the puzzle below.
Write one letter in each box.

Activity 25 continued

ACROSS

1. Used to show map distance vs. actual distance
6. Tops of mountains
10. A contour _____
11. Opposite of *won't*
12. A person who is between 13 and 19
14. Alphabetical _____
15. 12 months
17. Personal computer (abbreviation)
18. Looks like a small rounded mountain
20. I told you _____ !
21. Altitude
24. Past tense of *sit*
25. The Mediterranean _____
26. Opposite of *dry*
27. It changes every 15 degrees longitude.
28. Ontario (abbreviation)
29. Collection
30. Used to represent something on a map
33. A boy's name
36. Used to catch fish
38. The way from one place to another
39. Railroad (abbreviation)
41. Sometimes used to show elevation
45. They look like mountains without peaks.
46. A honey _____
47. Northwest (abbreviation)

DOWN

1. Upward or downward inclines
2. A great _____ route
3. Also
4. Robert E. _____
5. Halfway between two points
6. Lowland
7. Near to
8. Map legend
9. Look
13. National Aeronautics and Space Administration (abbreviation)
16. The earth _____ on its axis.
18. Houses
19. Opposite of *high*
22. The sun rises in the _____ .
23. Height from sea level
24. Past tense of *steal*
29. A mountainside that is not gentle
31. Spun wool
32. You find symbols _____ a map.
34. A third person pronoun
35. A restaurant food list
37. Some roads twist and _____ .
40. How to polish
42. Maine (abbreviation)
43. Exist
44. Southwest (abbreviation)

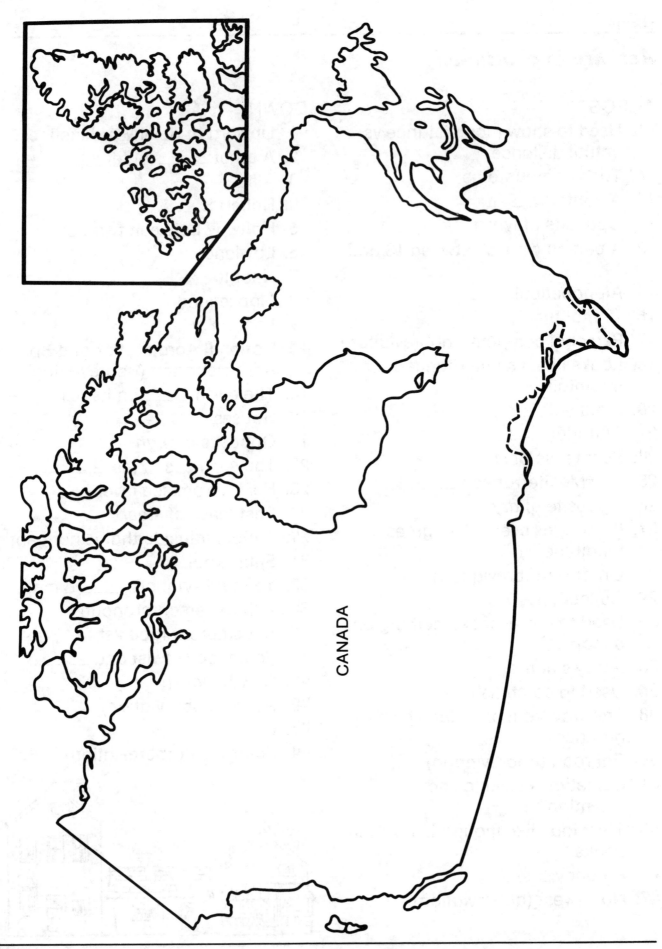

CANADA

Exploring Our World with Maps © 1988

PART III
Answer Key

Group Activity A

1. b	6. d	11. c
2. d	7. b	12. a
3. a	8. d	13. c
4. b	9. a	14. d
5. c	10. d	15. d

Group Activity B

1. a	6. d	11. a	16. a
2. c	7. c	12. d	17. d
3. a	8. a	13. b	18. d
4. d	9. b	14. c	19. a
5. b	10. b	15. b	20. b

Group Activity C

1. c	6. a	11. b	16. b
2. a	7. c	12. d	17. c
3. a	8. b	13. b	18. a
4. c	9. d	14. d	19. b
5. d	10. b	15. a	20. c

Activity 1

1. b	5. a
2. c	6. d
3. a	7. d
4. d	8. a

Activity 2

1. a	4. a	7. a
2. c	5. b	8. c
3. b	6. b	9. c

Activity 3

Activity 4

1. b	5. c
2. a	6. b
3. d	7. b
4. c	

Activity 5

1. trees	4. one
2. park	5. no
3. lake	

Activity 6

1. b	4. c	7. d
2. d	5. a	8. c
3. a	6. a	9. b

Activity 7

1. b	6. c
2. b	7. b
3. a	8. d
4. a	9. a
5. d	10. b

Activity 8

1. b	6. d	11. c
2. d	7. b	12. c
3. a	8. a	13. d
4. d	9. b	14. c
5. d	10. b	

Activity 9

NORTH

school
house 2
house 4

WEST			EAST
house 2	Intersection of Star Lake Road and Route 23	school	
church		house 4	
house 1		house 3	
		hospital	

house 3
hospital
church
house 1

SOUTH

Activity 10

Activity 11

1. a	5. b	9. b
2. c	6. c	10. a
3. b	7. a	11. d
4. c	8. c	12. c

Activity 12

1. b	7. d
2. d	8. a
3. b	9. b
4. c	10. d
5. a	11. c
6. a	

12.

	Ash	Box	Cushing	Downs	Elk	Garden City
Ash		30	70	70	50	30
Box	30		45	100	80	60
Cushing	70	45		65	60	40
Downs	70	100	65		20	40
Elk	50	80	60	20		20
Garden City	30	60	40	40	20	

Activity 13

1. a	5. a	9. a
2. d	6. d	10. c
3. c	7. c	11. a
4. a	8. a	12. a

Activity 14

1. d	5. d	9. d
2. a	6. b	10. b
3. d	7. a	11. c
4. b	8. c	12. d

Activity 15

Activity 16

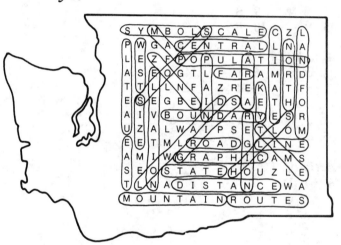

Activity 17

1. a	5. a	9. d
2. d	6. b	10. c
3. c	7. b	11. d
4. c	8. c	

Activity 18

A.
1. Kansas	10. Illinois
2. Connecticut	11. New Mexico
3. Alabama	12. Rhode Island
4. Montana	13. Arizona
5. Nevada	14. Oklahoma
6. Idaho	15. Washington
7. Oregon	16. Texas
8. Delaware	17. Wisconsin
9. Massachusetts	

B.
1. Central and Mountain Time
2. Eastern Time
3. Central Time
4. Mountain Time
5. Pacific Time
6. Mountain and Pacific Time
7. Pacific and Mountain Time
8. Eastern Time
9. Eastern Time
10. Central Time
11. Mountain Time
12. Eastern Time
13. Mountain Time
14. Central Time
15. Pacific Time
16. Central and Mountain Time
17. Central Time

Activity 19
1. D
2. A
3. C
4. C
5. B
6. F
7. C
8. E
9. B
10. E

Activity 20
1. c
2. d
3. a
4. b
5. c
6. a
7. d
8. b
9. a
10. b
11. d
12. a
13. c
14. a

Activity 21
A.
1. D
2. C
3. B
4. E
5. A
6. F

B.
1. B
2. E
3. D
4. C
5. A

Activity 22
1. a
2. b
3. d
4. a
5. c
6. b
7. a
8. a
9. c
10. b
11. a
12. d
13. a
14. d
15. c
16. c
17. d
18. b
19. b
20. a

Activity 23
1. b
2. a
3. b
4. b
5. d
6. c
7. d

8.

Activity 24
1. c
2. b
3. b
4. b
5. c
6. a
7. a
8. c
9. c
10. d
11. c
12. d
13. b
14. c

Activity 25

PART IV
Maps and Photos

Map 1   Map of an Imaginary School

North

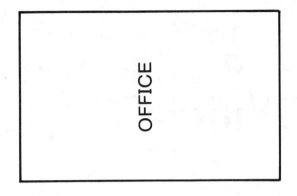

OFFICE

BATH-ROOMS NURSE

TEACHER'S ROOM

AUDITORIUM

ROOM 6

ROOM 5

ROOM 9

ROOM 8

ROOM 12

ROOM 11

ROOM 2

ROOM 1

ROOM 4

ROOM 3

ROOM 7

LIBRARY

ROOM 10

JANITOR

Exploring Our World with Maps © 1988

Map 2   Map of an Imaginary Town Neighborhood

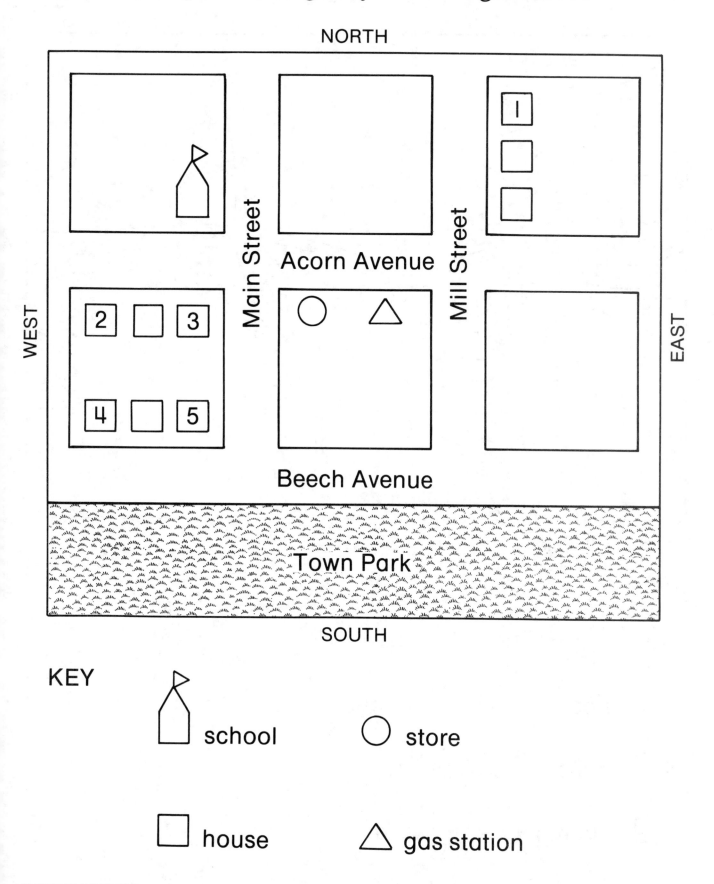

NORTH

WEST

EAST

Main Street

Acorn Avenue

Mill Street

2   3

4   5

Beech Avenue

Town Park

SOUTH

KEY

school   ◯ store

☐ house   △ gas station

Map 3   Map of an Imaginary Country Neighborhood

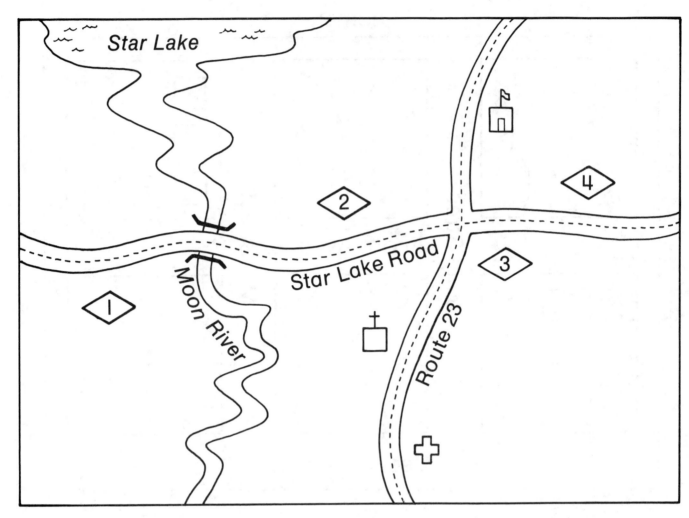

1 inch = 1 mile

KEY

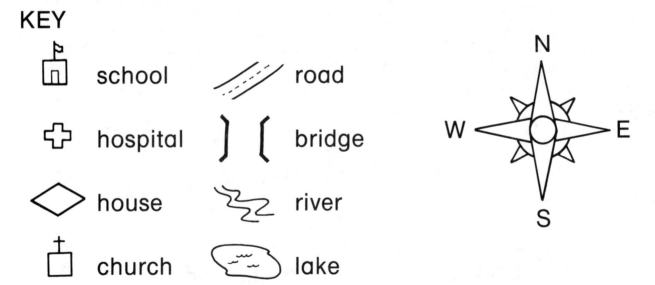

- school
- hospital
- house
- church

- road
- bridge
- river
- lake

Map 4

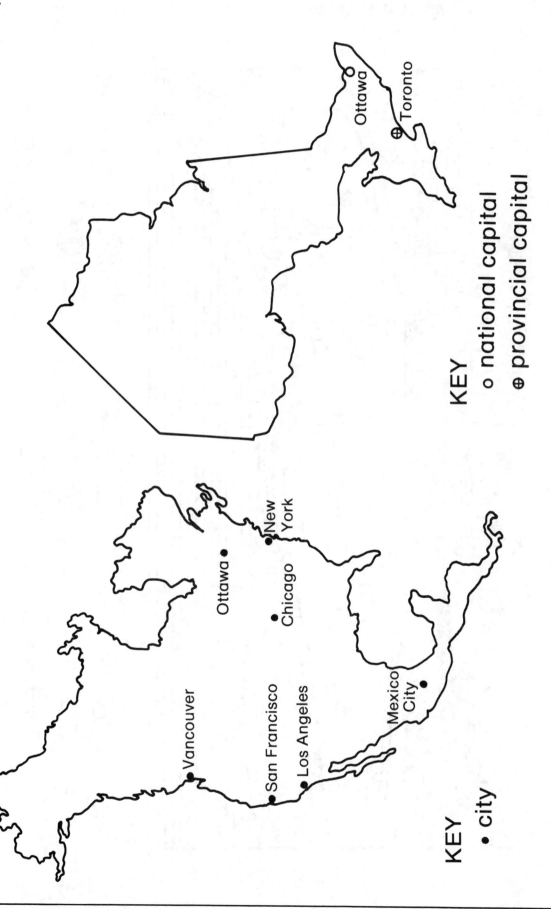

Map A   Outline Map of North America

Map B   Outline Map of Ontario Province

Vancouver

Ottawa

San Francisco
Los Angeles

Chicago

New York

Mexico City

KEY
• city

Ottawa

Toronto

KEY
o national capital
⊕ provincial capital

Map 5   **Map of a Photo**

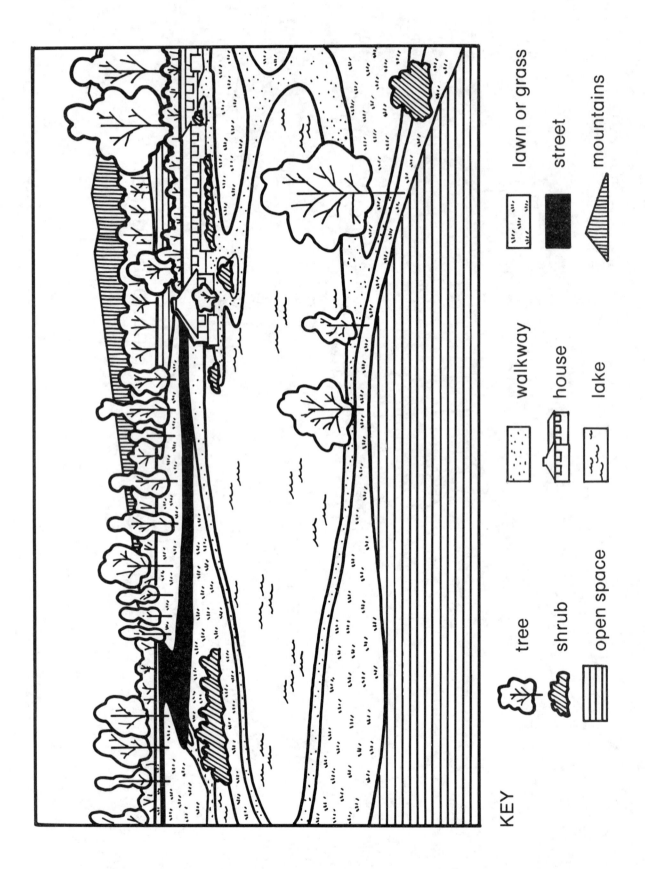

KEY

tree   walkway   lawn or grass

shrub   house   street

open space lake   mountains

Map 6

Map A   Road Map of Chad City Area

KEY

- interstate highway
- U.S. highway
- state highway
- town or city

1″ = 20 miles

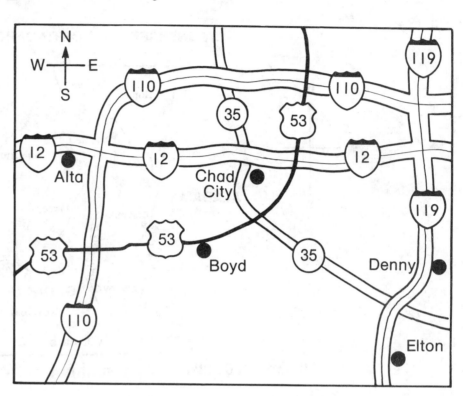

Map B   Road Map of Dream City Area

KEY

- interstate highway
- U.S. highway
- state highway
- town or city

1″ = 20 miles

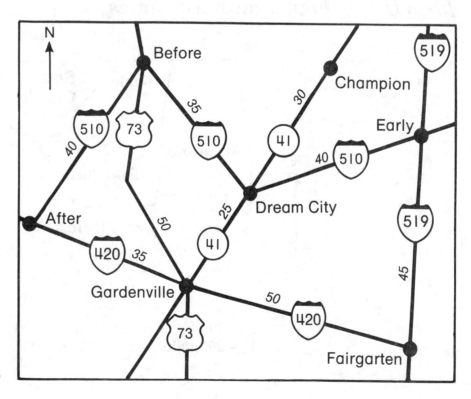

Map 7

Map A   Some Cities and Rivers in Georgia

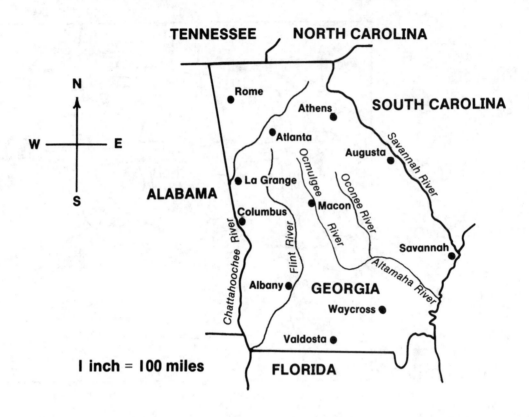

1 inch = 100 miles

Map B   Four Southern States

1" = 200 miles

Exploring Our World with Maps © 1988

Map 8 **The Western United States**

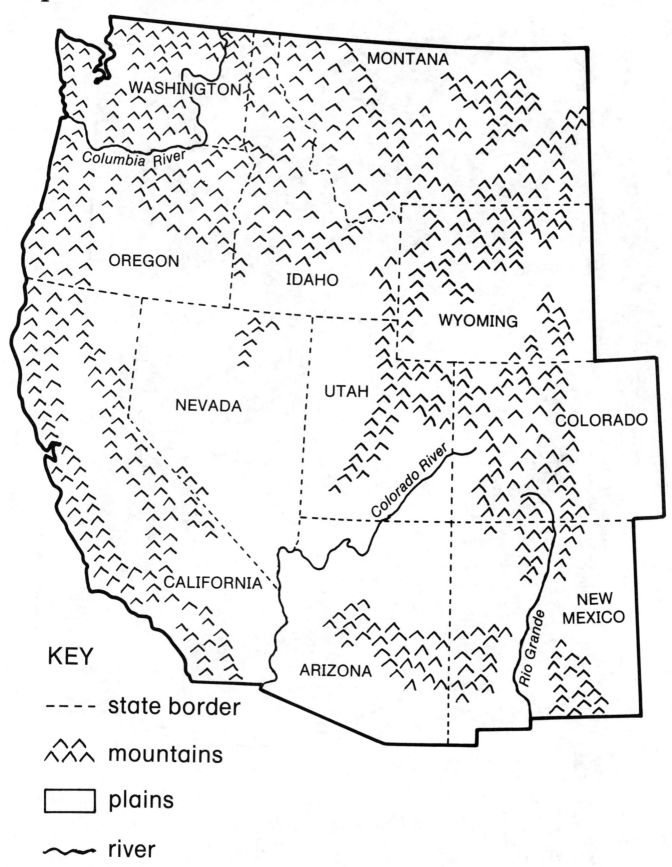

KEY

- - - - state border

⋀⋀⋀ mountains

▭ plains

⁓ river

Map 9   The Western United States

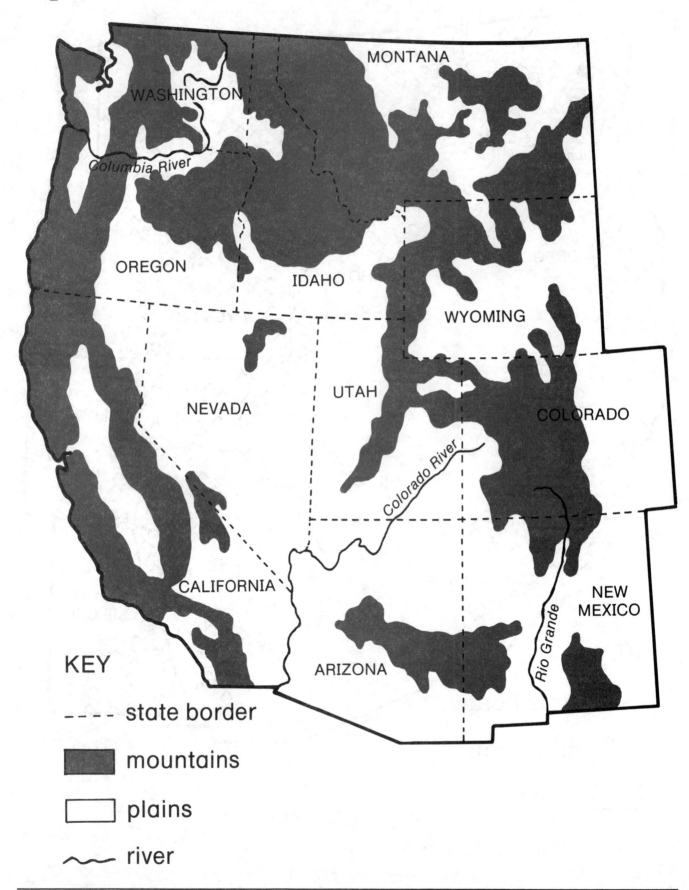

KEY

- - - - state border

▨ mountains

□ plains

〜 river

Map 10   **Political Map of the United States**

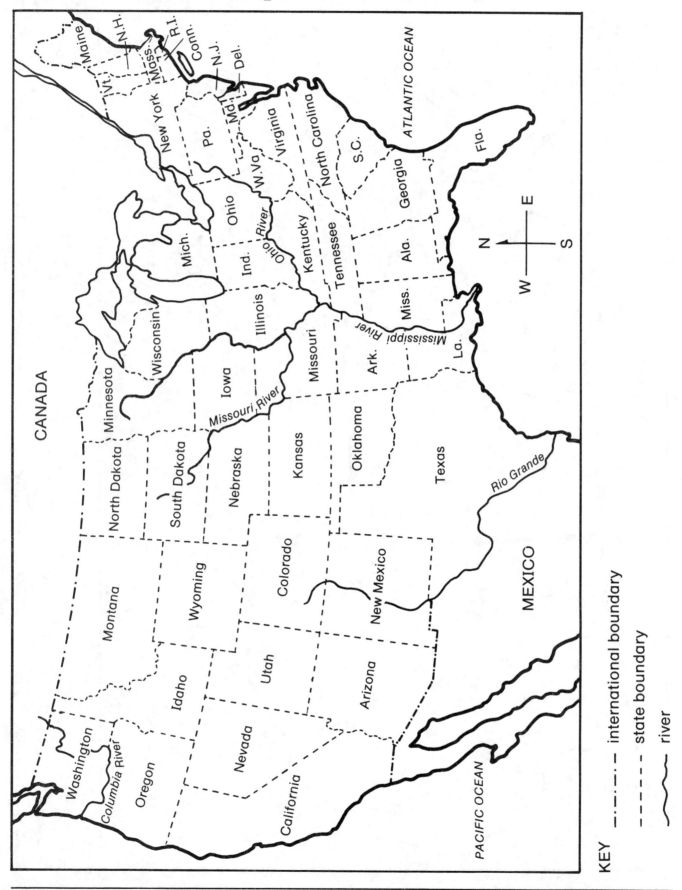

Map 11   Regional Map of the United States

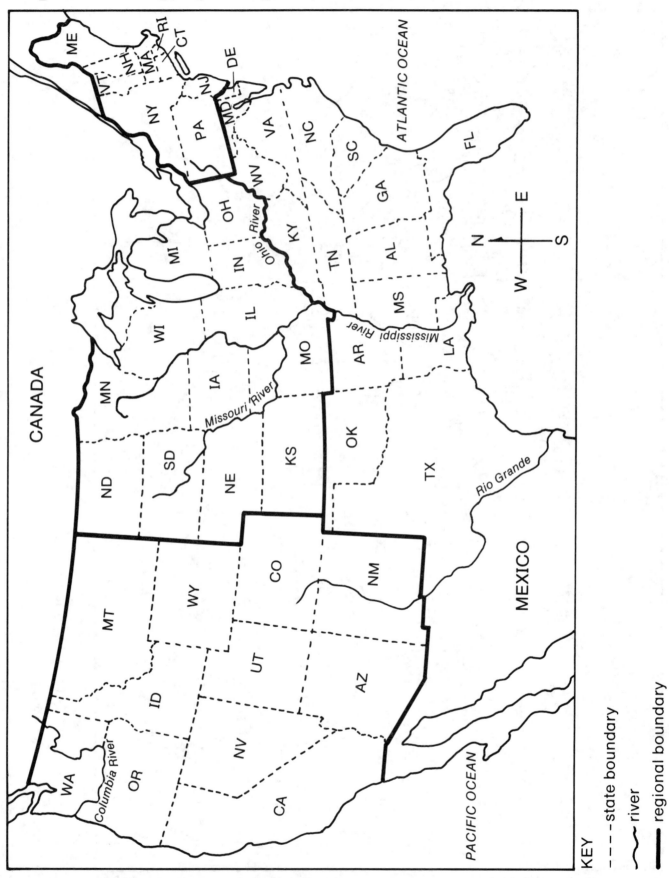

Exploring Our World with Maps © 1988

Map 12   Some Highways and Cities in Iowa

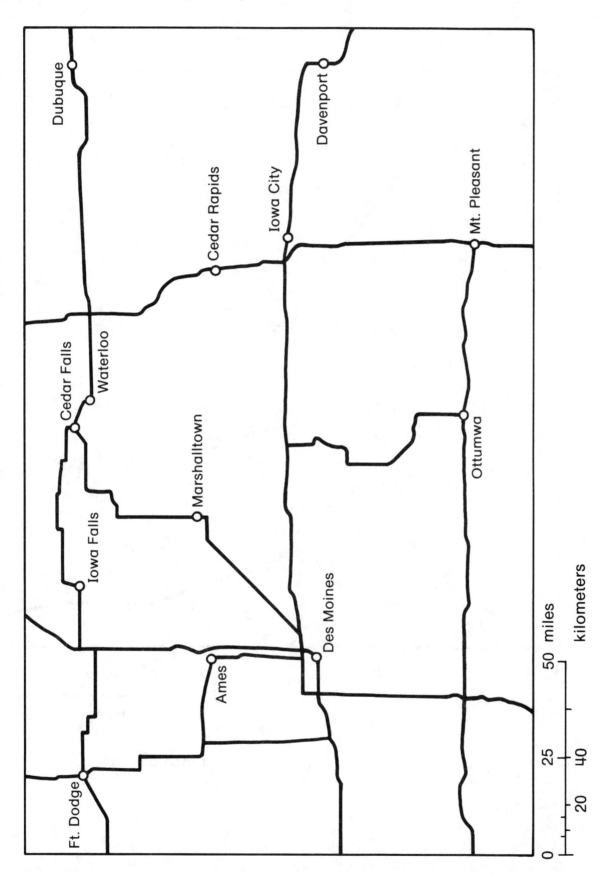

Map 13   Road Map of the Happydale Area

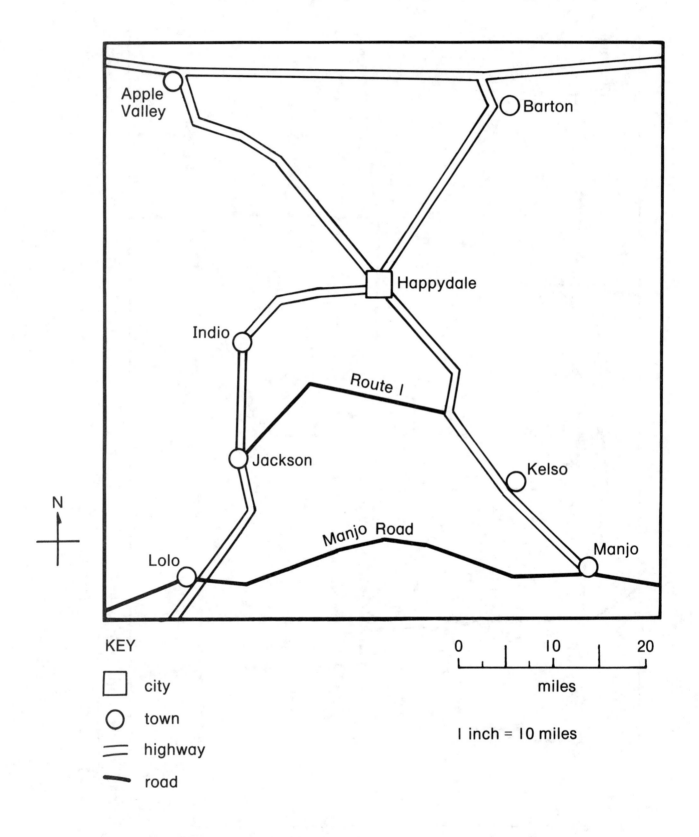

KEY

☐ city

○ town

═ highway

▬ road

0   10   20

miles

1 inch = 10 miles

Map 14   United States Time Zones

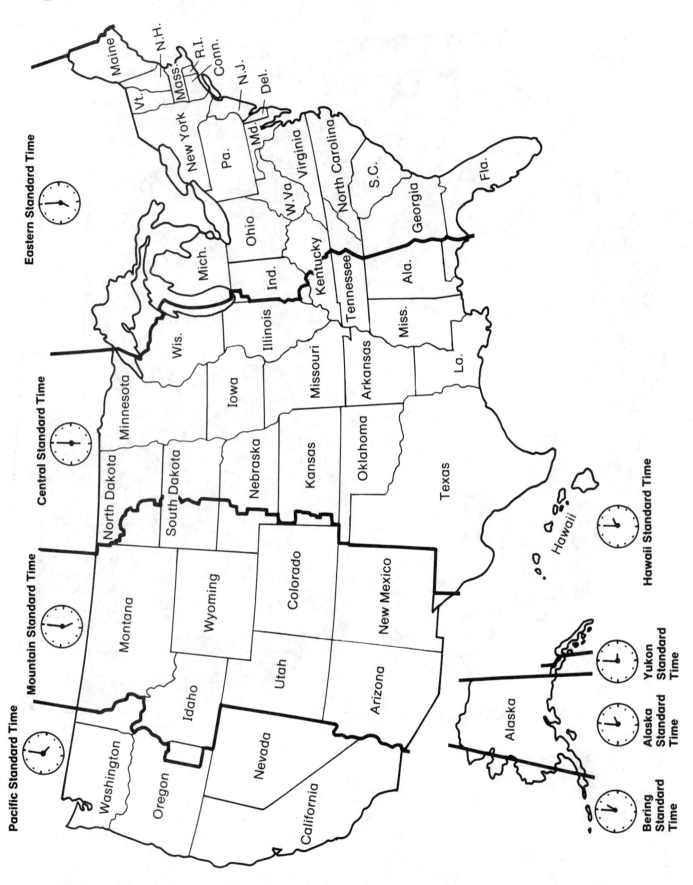

Map 15

Physical Map of the Western United States

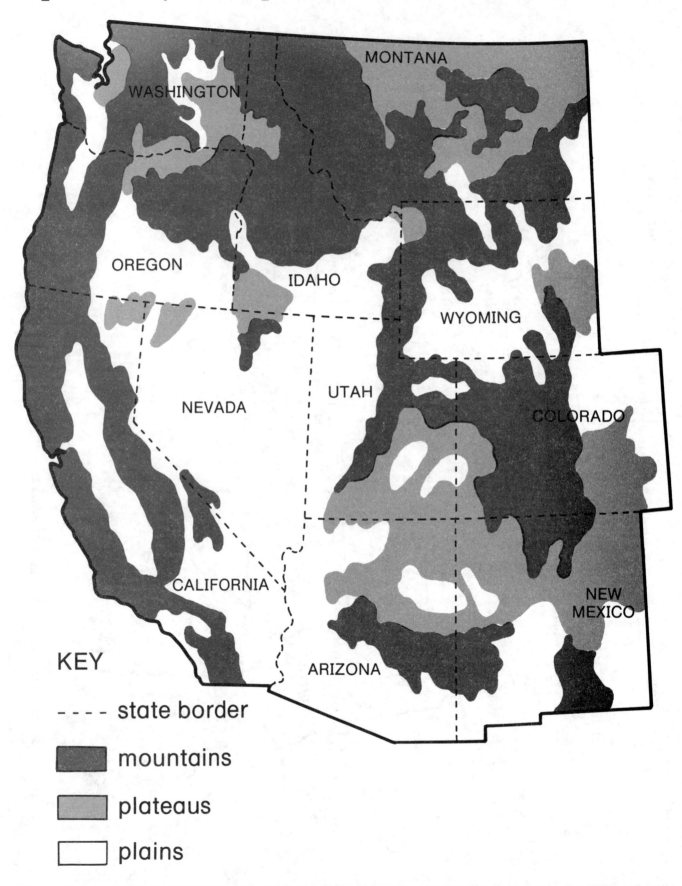

MONTANA

WASHINGTON

OREGON

IDAHO

WYOMING

NEVADA

UTAH

COLORADO

CALIFORNIA

ARIZONA

NEW MEXICO

KEY

- - - - state border

mountains

plateaus

plains

Exploring Our World with Maps © 1988

Map 16   Populations of Some Major United States Metropolitan Areas

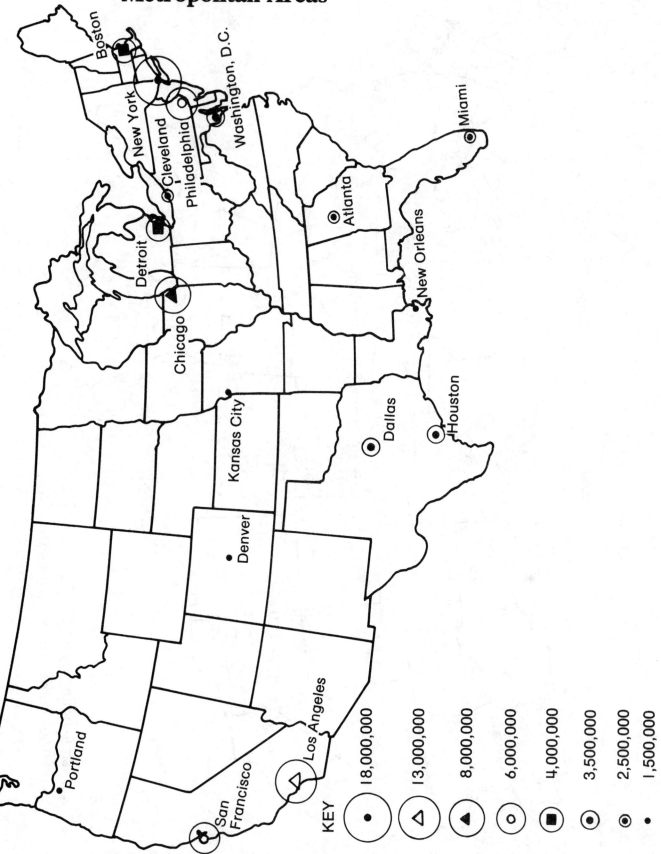

KEY

18,000,000	⦿
13,000,000	◁
8,000,000	◀
6,000,000	◎
4,000,000	▣
3,500,000	⊙
2,500,000	◉
1,500,000	•

Map 17   Wheat Production in the United States

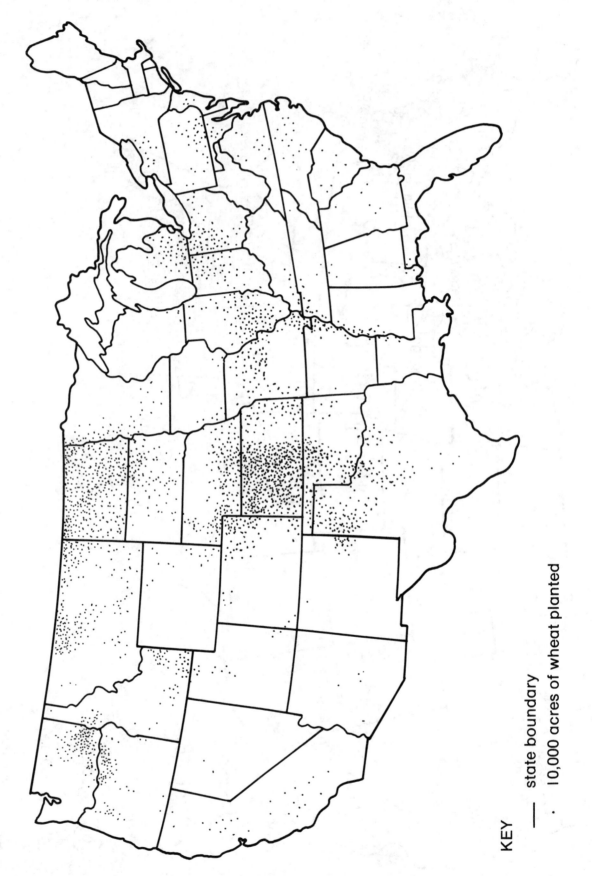

KEY

—— state boundary

· 10,000 acres of wheat planted

Map 18

Yearly Precipitation in the United States

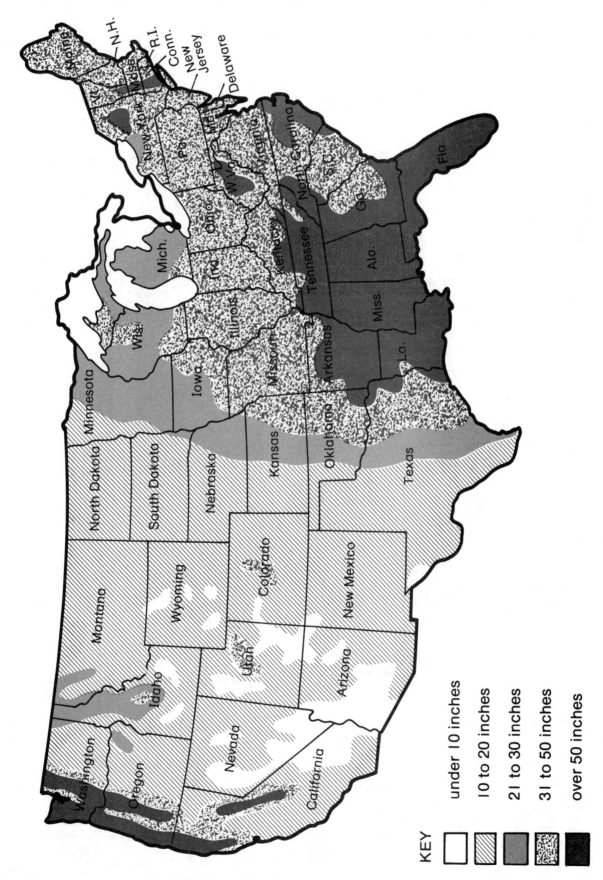

KEY

☐ under 10 inches

▨ 10 to 20 inches

▨ 21 to 30 inches

▨ 31 to 50 inches

■ over 50 inches

Map 19

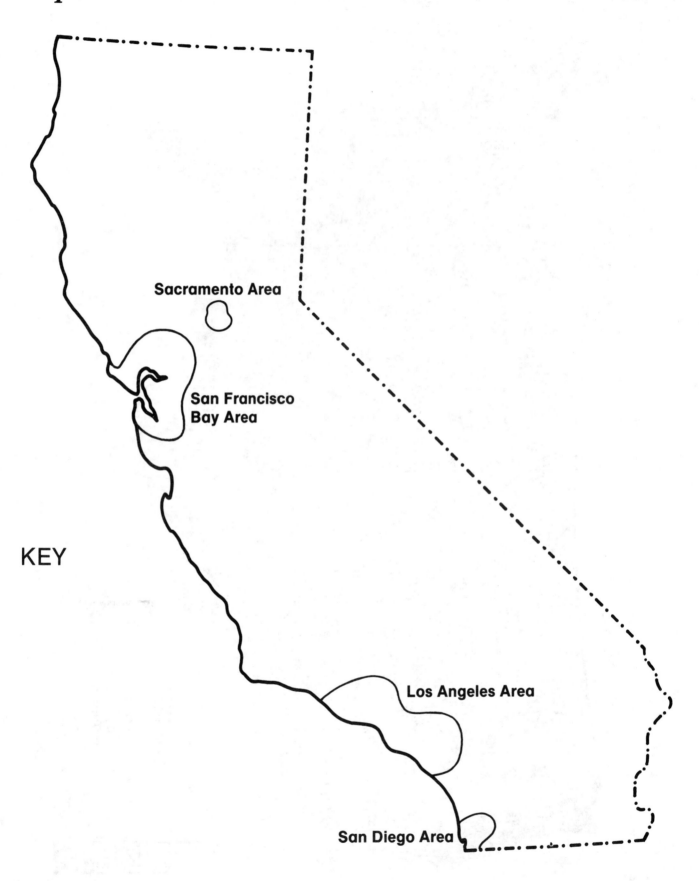

KEY

Sacramento Area

San Francisco
Bay Area

Los Angeles Area

San Diego Area

Map 20
Map A   The Western Hemisphere

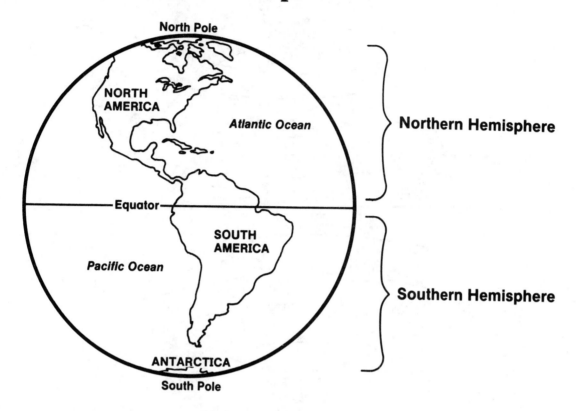

Map B   The Eastern Hemisphere

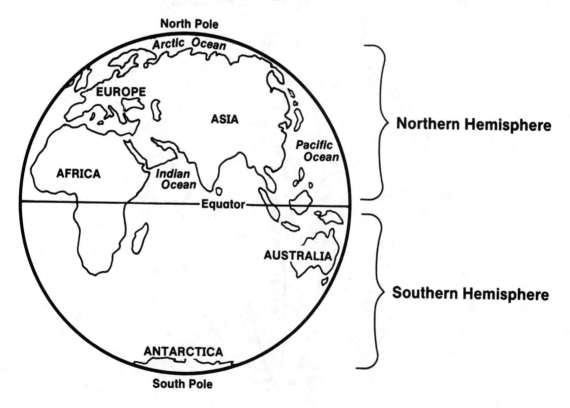

Map 21

Map A   **Lines of Latitude (Parallels)**

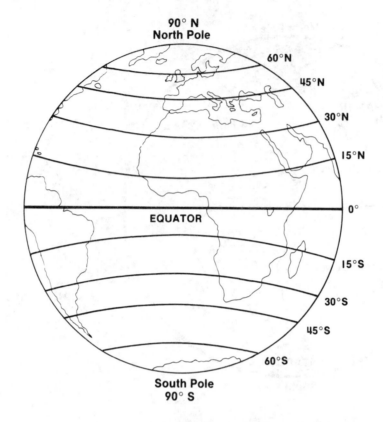

Map B   **Lines of Longitude (Meridians)**

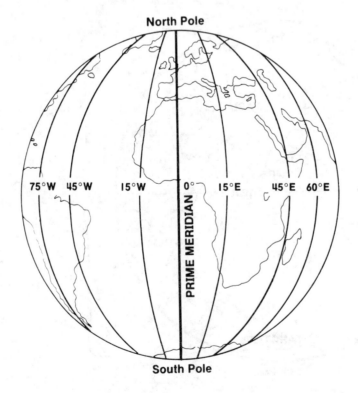

Map 22   **Cities Around the World**

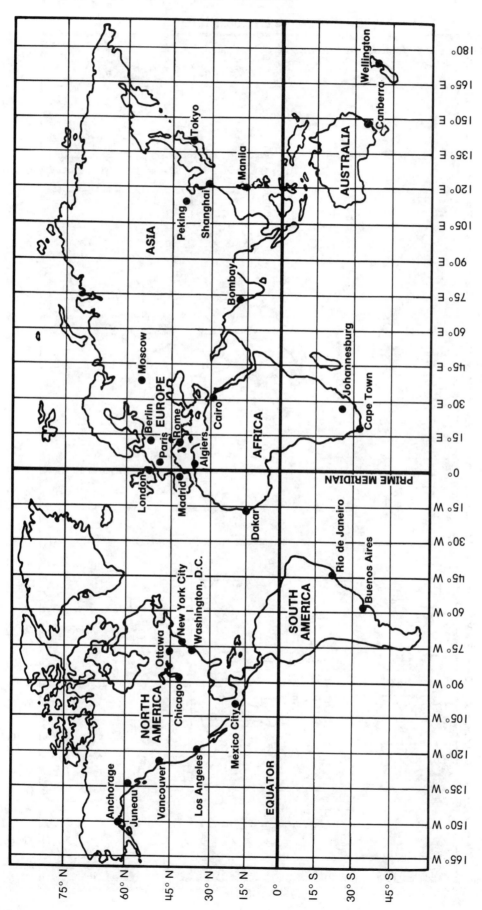

Map 23   World Time Zones

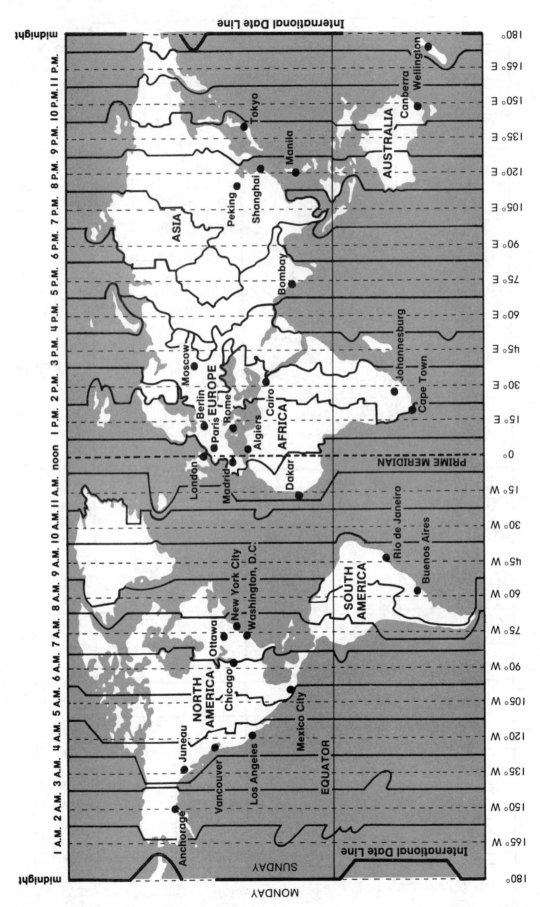

Map 24

Map A   A Polar Projection Map

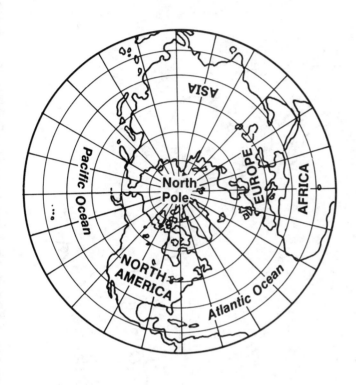

Map B   Mercator Projection Map

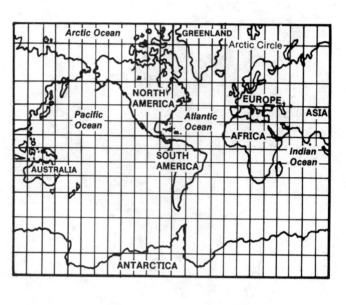

Map C   Lambert's Projection Map

Map D   Interrupted Projection Map

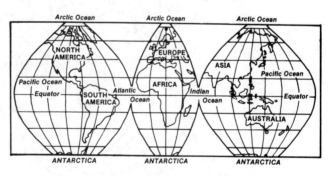

Map 25

Map A   **Yearly Rainfall in South America**

Map B   **Mexico's Major Metal Areas**

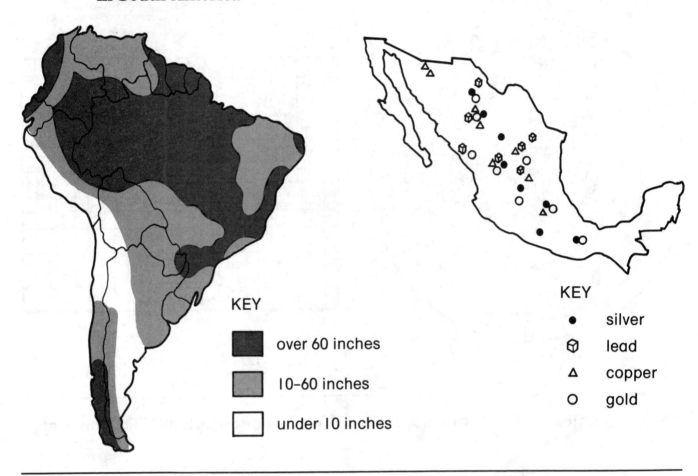

KEY

▪ over 60 inches

▪ 10–60 inches

☐ under 10 inches

KEY

● silver

⬡ lead

△ copper

○ gold

Map C   **Topological Map of Elbert's Mountain**

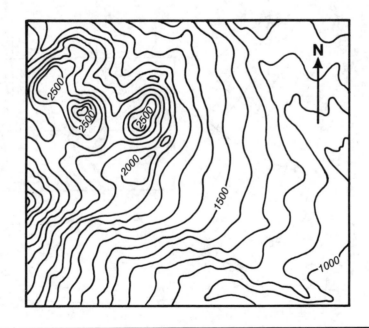

Exploring Our World with Maps © 1988

Map 26   **A Map of a Zoo**

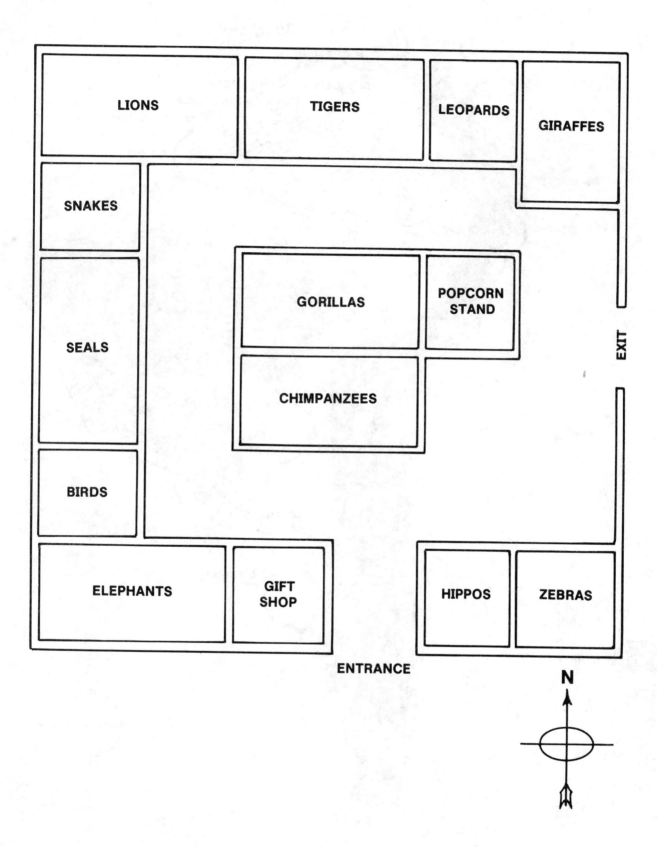

Map 27   **Landforms of South America**

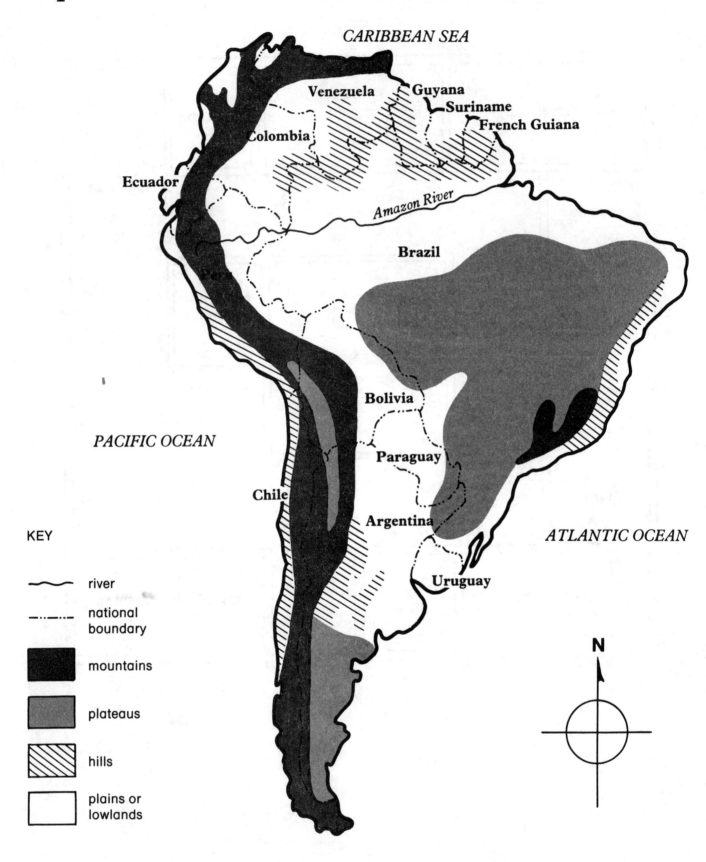

CARIBBEAN SEA

Venezuela   Guyana
             Suriname
Colombia   French Guiana

Ecuador

Amazon River

Peru

Brazil

PACIFIC OCEAN

Bolivia

Paraguay

Chile

Argentina   ATLANTIC OCEAN

Uruguay

KEY

～～～ river

—·—·— national
       boundary

▉ mountains

▨ plateaus

▧ hills

☐ plains or
   lowlands

N

Photo 1

Photo 2

Exploring Our World with Maps © 1988

Photo 3

Photo 4